Arts: A Second Level Course

The Age of Revolutions   Units 25-27

Beethoven

Prepared by Owain Edwards for the Course Team

The Open University Press

The Open University Press
Walton Hall Bletchley Bucks

First published 1972

Designed by the Media Development Group of the Open University.

Printed in Great Britain by
EYRE AND SPOTTISWOODE LIMITED
AT GROSVENOR PRESS PORTSMOUTH

SBN 335 00572 1

This text forms part of the correspondence element of an Open University Second Level Course. The complete list of units in the course is given at the end of this text.

For general availability of supporting material referred to in this text, please write to the Director of Marketing, The Open University, Walton Hall, Bletchley, Bucks.

Further information on Open University courses may be obtained from the Admissions Office, The Open University, P.O. Box 48, Bletchley, Bucks.

CONTENTS

INTRODUCTION

It is not the fact that Beethoven's life span (1770–1827) coincides with the period of the Age of Revolutions Course which made him an obvious choice for study. The music of Mozart and Haydn was being played throughout Europe at this time, but it is in Beethoven's, not theirs, that we recognize the spirit of radical change. Beethoven was the revolutionary figure in music from the end of the eighteenth century.

You have *three* weeks to work through these units.

Our aim is to move forward on two fronts:

1 to present significant biographical detail;
2 through asking you to listen to a selection of Beethoven's music, both on gramophone records and in the broadcasts, to enable you to become familiar with his style, and *to get the feel of his music.*

I hope that you'll find the exercises, based on the music on record, useful in reinforcing the habit of listening perceptively, or, possibly, in introducing you to the practice of giving the whole of your attention to music. The exercises will also give you practice in learning to read music. If you cannot read music now, however, there is no need to be intimidated by the pages of music in this text. You ought to be able to manage perfectly well without being able to read music as long as you listen carefully. I have included the scores of a few movements in order to give students who do read music the means of noticing more, perhaps, than they might otherwise have been aware of simply from listening. Reading and understanding these scores is not essential for this course. Regard them as a bonus meant for your use later, if you can't read music now. Obviously, it is to your advantage to learn as soon as you can, if you are interested in music.

It is useful in fact, *not* to look at the scores even if you do read music while answering the exercises, unless I have referred you to them specifically. This ensures that you have to listen very carefully to pick up the points of detail in context.

Preparatory Reading

You may not have taken the Arts Foundation Course. I am assuming, nevertheless, that you have a knowledge of the rudiments of music. Otherwise, this study would need too many parenthetical definitions as we went along.

If you need to cover the groundwork, try and find a 'rudiments of music' book, and have it by you for reference while you are reading this (for the foundation course we recommended, Ottó Károlyi, *Introducing Music*, Penguin Books, 1965). The music units in the Arts Foundation Course are: Units 13–14, *Introduction to Music*, 27–28, *Mendelssohn's Rediscovery of Bach*, and there is also a music section in Units 15–16, *Form and Meaning*. If you have not studied music before it would certainly be an advantage for you to have seen the foundation course material before starting on *Beethoven*. On the other hand, if you have studied a practical aspect of music, singing or playing the piano for instance, and have taken this to a fairly advanced level of competence, you would not need to go over the rudiments and definitions presented in Units 13–14, but you *are* still recommended to look at *Form and Meaning* to learn about formal analysis in music, and *Mendelssohn* for an introduction to the discipline of musicology.

Gramophone Records and Books

Make sure you have the records to go with this text.

They play a vital part in the teaching of the units. As you read you will frequently be asked to put on a gramophone record and play band so and so. Omitting to play the music would mean having to pass over the exercises completely, since these are usually of the 'listen-and-respond' kind. Although it is easier to commit facts about Beethoven to memory than to hear, in the music, all the details I may be asking for in the exercises, do look further ahead than to the immediate requirements of this course! Your experience of music *in general* ought to be enriched through concentrating now for three weeks on Beethoven, and, by insisting that you do actually *listen* to the music, you may be forming a good habit for a lifetime.

Details of the contents of both records are printed on the back inside cover of this text.

You will need the two set books: *Beethoven, Impressions by his Contemporaries*, edited by O. G. Sonneck (published in Great Britain by Constable & Co. Ltd., in the United States by Dover Publications Inc. New York, 1967); and J. W. N. Sullivan, *Beethoven* (Allen & Unwin, 1964). If you are not able to follow up my references you won't get the emphasis intended. Reading these units alone, for example, without the balancing accounts in Sonneck and Sullivan, you would probably feel a disproportionate emphasis on the matter of Beethoven's deafness.

I have drawn on a variety of documents to try to bring over Beethoven as a living person in a particular kind of musical environment. His letters are a source of great fascination: almost 1,600 survive, of which the 180 most interesting ones have recently been published in *Selected letters of Beethoven* (trans. Emily Anderson, ed. Alan Tyson, London, Macmillan, 1967). I would recommend this book for further reading. To make it easier, therefore, for you to follow up my quotations from the letters, I have quoted as far as possible from letters included in this selection.

Broadcast Components

Radio

The first radio programme introduces Beethoven as the new kind of emancipated musician, a free *artist*. The speaker in this illustrated talk, Dr Alan Tyson, is concerned with placing Beethoven in a certain social context. You will also find that he makes clearer the relationship between these *Beethoven* units and the rest of the Age of Revolutions Course. In the second and third radio programmes Professor Joseph Kerman examines Beethoven's role as a revolutionary in music. Details are provided in the booklet of Supplementary Material relating to these units.

Television

The television programme comes in the second week of this three-week block and is a view of the slow movement of Beethoven *Piano Trio op. 70 no. 1*, '*The Ghost*'. Before you watch this you should have familiarized yourself with the music and attempted the exercise on page 64. The programme provides the central piece of critical analysis in these music units and supplies a full answer to the exercise based on this slow movement.

The members of the trio illustrating my analysis are: Geoffrey Buckley, free-lance soloist and resident pianist at the University College of Wales, Aberystwyth – he is also the pianist on the SECOND BEETHOVEN RECORD; Dennis Nesbitt, free-lance solo cellist, director of The Elizabethan Consort of Viols and professor at the Royal Academy of Music; and Clarence Myerscough, free-lance soloist and professor of violin at the Royal Academy of Music.

You may be interested to know that the piano is by Bösendorfer of Vienna, made in 1970. The violin was made by Maggini of Brescia, in about 1600, the cello by Stradivari at Cremona in 1714.

Assignment

Details of this are given in the booklet of Supplementary Material. Note that you should complete your assignment at the end of week 26 of the course, although you are not expected to have worked through the whole of Units 25–27 at that time.

Acknowledgements

I want to thank several people for help with these units: Alan Tyson, All Souls College, Oxford, and Joseph Kerman, Heather Professor of Music, University of Oxford (who both contributed invaluably to the block with their radio talks) for reading the units and offering helpful advice; colleagues in the Faculty of Arts of the Open University, especially Dinah Barsham, Trevor Bray, Donald Burrows, John Ferguson, Ossie Hanfling, Gerald Hendrie, Arnold Kettle, Philip Olleson, Derek Rowntree, for comments; Richard Callanan and John Selwyn Gilbert (BBC) for their part in producing the radio and television programmes; Tony Coulson (Library) for advice on the choice of illustrations; and Jill Bryant for secretarial expertise in preparing my manuscript for publication. I'd like also to thank the ten students who kindly read a draft of the units and let me have their comments on them.

SECTION 1   AN OUTLINE OF BEETHOVEN'S LIFE

Ludwig van Beethoven's exact date of birth is not known but records show that he was baptized on 17 December 1770. His father and grandfather, both musicians, were employed in Bonn at the court chapel of the ecclesiastical Elector of Cologne. His grandfather, Ludwig, was well thought of: having started in the chapel as a singer he had risen to the position of *Kapellmeister*, with direction of all the music at the Elector's court, which in addition to the chapel choir included a small orchestra. He was still alive and working as *Kapellmeister* when Beethoven was born to Maria Magdalena, his son Johann's wife.

Johann sang tenor in the choir, had an undistinguished career and ended up by being relieved of his post. Nevertheless, he recognized his son's aptitude for music and gave it encouragement from an early age: he taught him the harpsichord and violin, and had him performing in public by the age of seven. Talent in the shape of an infant prodigy was a saleable commodity. When Mozart (born 1756) was only six he had been exhibited around central Europe on two international concert tours, and had already written his first keyboard pieces the previous year (with father Leopold possibly guiding his pen). The young Beethoven made a slightly later start and, lacking perhaps the precocity as well as the most effective early training and a sufficiently ambitious vision on his father's part, was not to achieve celebrity as an infant prodigy.

Beethoven had his first training in music from his father but his most influential teacher as a boy was Christian Gottlob Neefe (1748–98) composer, court organist and director of the National Theatre in Bonn, who settled in the city in 1779. Besides teaching Beethoven the organ and piano and in particular introducing him to the *Forty-Eight Preludes and Fugues* of Johann Sebastian Bach, Neefe supervised his compositions. The first one Beethoven had published, a set of *Nine variations for piano on a march by Dressler*, appeared when he was twelve, notwithstanding the assertion on the title-page that the variations had been composed 'par un jeune Amateur Louis van Betthoven [sic] âgé de dix ans'.

Beethoven was deputizing at the organ for Neefe from eleven years of age, having abandoned all other studies in favour of music. At thirteen, on his appointment as Neefe's assistant organist, he joined his father as a musician at court. His duties also involved directing on occasion rehearsals of the small court orchestra, and playing the harpsichord in the orchestra in opera performances at the Elector's theatre. The orchestra was disbanded in 1784 but when a new opera company was established four years later Beethoven took his place in the orchestra as a viola player. He was gaining fluency in composition and experience in a wide field of music, including teaching, from which he supplemented his income.

In 1787 at the age of sixteen he was sent to Vienna, probably in the hope that he might get lessons from Mozart, but after only a fortnight there he had news from home that his mother was dying, and returned immediately. He felt his mother's untimely death very keenly. She was only forty. Beethoven had been more closely attached to her than to any other member of his family.

His father Johann van Beethoven took to drinking so heavily after this that he was soon unable to perform his duties satisfactorily at court. Two years later he was dismissed and, by what was a very humane arrangement, part of the salary he used to receive was paid to his son Ludwig, who at the age of eighteen was made legal head of the family. He had two younger brothers to care for; four other children in the family had previously died.

In 1787 Beethoven struck up a friendship with Count Ferdinand Ernst von Waldstein (1762–1823), eight years his senior and himself a trained musician. A lifelong patron of Beethoven's, he is remembered particularly as the one to whom Beethoven's op. 53 piano sonata in C major (the *Waldstein* Sonata) was dedicated in 1805.

Beethoven became acquainted with the literature and ideas of the time particularly through associating with the family of Helene von Breuning, widow of a former state counsellor, who had three sons and a daughter, Eleonore, for whom Beethoven's feelings were very warm. In this company he encountered in particular the work of Goethe, Schiller and Kant, and the ideals of social conscience and democracy about which he was to show such strong feelings. At that time, when Marie-Antoinette's brother, Emperor Joseph II of Austria died in 1790 Beethoven wrote a dramatic cantata mourning his death. (You will recall reading about Joseph II of Austria earlier in the Age of Revolutions Course, where he is referred to as an 'Enlightened Despot' on account of his humanitarian legislation and religious toleration – see Unit 1, Section 3.5, pp. 38–42.)

The two outstanding composers of this time were Mozart (1756–91) and Haydn (1732–1809). Beethoven is said to have played for Mozart in 1787. Haydn he probably first met in 1790 when Haydn was passing through Bonn at Christmas, on his way to England. The Elector honoured Haydn by arranging the performance of one of the composer's Masses in church, and the same warm hospitality was shown on his return in 1792. On that occasion, probably after seeing Beethoven's *Cantata on the Death of Joseph II*, Haydn gave him encouragement and also the ambition to study under him. Mozart had died in 1791 leaving Haydn the greatest living composer. In so far as people thought in those terms at all, Haydn had been more famous than Mozart even before Mozart's death. In 1792 Beethoven obtained leave of absence from the musical establishment at court to complete his musical training under Haydn in Vienna.

The following extracts are from documents dating from that time.

1 *Count Waldstein's parting inscription in Beethoven's album*

Dear Beethoven!
You are going to Vienna in fulfillment of your long-frustrated wishes. The Genius of Mozart is mourning and weeping over the death of her pupil. She found a refuge but no occupation with the inexhaustible Haydn; through him she wishes to form a union with another. With the help of assiduous labour you shall receive Mozart's spirit from Haydn's hands . . .
Bonn, the 29th October 1792. Your true friend Waldstein.

(A. W. Thayer, *Life of Beethoven*, revised and ed. Elliot Forbes, Princeton University Press, 1967, p. 115.)

2 *From the Berliner Musik Zeitung of 26 October 1793*

In November of last year Ludwig van Beethoven, Assistant Court Organist and now unquestionably one of the foremost piano-players, went to Vienna at the expense of our Elector in order to perfect himself further, under Haydn's direction, in the art of composition.

(H. C. Robbins Landon, *Beethoven*, London, Thames and Hudson, 1970, pp. 55, 57.)

From these extracts one gets an impression of the very high regard in which Haydn was held, and of the great promise Beethoven was felt to have. It is interesting how the step was regarded in terms of a musical apostolic succession, of Beethoven going to receive the spirit of Mozart *from the hands* of Haydn, and it underlines how in the eighteenth century the musician was still regarded as a craftsman: the aristocratic patron recognizing the traditional concept of genius being handed down from the master craftsman to his pupil.

It was a decisive step, taken at a fortunate time. Two years later it could have been more hazardous: the French armies invaded Bonn and the Elector fled. In 1795 Beethoven's brothers Karl and Johann left Bonn to join Beethoven in Vienna. By 1797 the French republic had been extended to include the Electorate of Cologne. If Beethoven ever had felt himself under an obligation to return to the court at Bonn, after finishing his studies, the decision was now taken out of his hands. His post no longer existed. He never returned to Bonn.

But Haydn was not the teacher to bring the best out of such a headstrong pupil: he was not enough of a disciplinarian. While continuing therefore to show his exercises to Haydn, Beethoven found a sterner teacher in the opera director Johann Schenk (1761–1836), and when Haydn went on his second visit to London in 1794, his period as Haydn's (nominal) pupil ended naturally. Hoping to improve his technique as a composer, Beethoven took lessons from another musician of Haydn's generation, the *Kapellmeister* to St Stephen's Cathedral, Johann Georg Albrechtsberger (1736–1809). This Viennese musician was distinguished both as a theorist and as a counterpoint teacher. Counterpoint was a skill Beethoven felt he needed to acquire. His studies in counterpoint under Albrechtsberger lasted about a year.

It was characteristic of Beethoven that although he obviously felt the need to have a thorough training in the difficult disciplines of music, placing himself under the direction of three teachers shortly after arriving in Vienna, he strongly resisted being disciplined. Putting it another way, it might be said that Beethoven needed the experience of being told the official party line at first hand by the leaders, to strengthen his conviction in himself, even though others might object to his music. There wasn't a *party line* of course; rather, a development of certain conventions in music with which Beethoven was not inclined to conform – certainly not simply for the sake of being conventional.

By 1795 he had had enough of such instruction. He preferred from then on to rely on his intuitive musicality than on the advice of more experienced musicians, although three years later he started taking advice on the setting of Italian words to music from Antonio Salieri (1750–1825), a famous operatic composer and *Kapellmeister* to the Imperial Court. He honoured Salieri by dedicating to him three sonatas for piano and violin, op. 12, and Haydn with the dedication of his brilliant op. 2 piano sonatas. He respected Haydn greatly,

Figure 1 Antonio Salieri (1750–1825), an anonymous portrait in oils (Gesellschaft der Musikfreunde, Vienna).

Figure 2 Joseph Haydn (1732–1809), portrait in oils by Thomas Hardy, 1791 (Royal College of Music, London).

Figure 3 Wolfgang Amadeus Mozart (1756–91), unfinished portrait by Joseph Lange, c. 1790 (Mozarteum, Saltzburg).

more so perhaps later when he was no longer his pupil, but it is said that he refused to comply with a request that he put on his compositions 'pupil of Haydn', since he felt that he had learned nothing from him.

Beethoven lived during the first few months in Vienna on the allowance he had from the Elector of Cologne, but this was stopped the following January. When he wrote in November begging financial assistance from the Elector, his letter being accompanied by a petition on his behalf from Haydn, along with five compositions to show his progress, his request was refused. Four of the pieces had been recognized as having been written before he had left Bonn, and it was suggested that as he was heading for financial trouble he should return there. But despite a temporary shortage of money, Beethoven landed on his feet in Vienna and he was never to suffer the poverty into which Mozart had sunk before his death. In fact, he earned quite well – but he managed his affairs so badly that he was often reduced to worrying about money matters. How right he was about his ability to deal with money, when he wrote to the publisher Franz Anton Hoffmeister (1754–1812) of Leipzig, 'The only currency I can cope with is Viennese ducats. How much that sum amounts to in your thalers and gulden does not concern me, because I am really an incompetent business man who is bad at arithmetic' (*Selected letters of Beethoven*, p. 26). And sadly, during the last twenty years of his life when his income ought to have been more than adequate, he lived in a state of squalor.

Besides treating these early years in Vienna as an opportunity for intense study in composition, Beethoven was making his mark as a performer in the aristocratic circle to which he had gained admission. His public début as a pianist was made in the grand manner. He appeared as soloist in a charity concert in aid of musicians' widows and orphans. This was a high-society occasion held with all splendour at the National Theatre on 29 March 1795.

Although he was to include in his programme a concerto of his own composition, later to be published as *Piano Concerto No. 2 in B flat*, the advertisements, printed in German and Italian, put the emphasis entirely on his ability as a great *performer* (indicated by '*Meister* Herrn Ludwig . . .' 'Il Sigre. Maestro Ludovico de Beethoven'), and in the report of the concert in the *Wiener Zeitung* he is called the 'famous Mr. Beethoven'. Vienna accepted him with acclaim. He did not have to fight his way up, he had arrived at the top and was acknowledged to be the greatest pianist in Europe. To have made this impact so early, Beethoven must have been performing in private parties, and gossip had taken his reputation abroad. For a time he lodged in the same building as Prince Karl Lichnowsky (1756–1814). The prince, an accomplished musician, had been a patron of Mozart as well as his pupil and travelling companion in 1789 on a concert tour to Prague, Dresden, Leipzig and Berlin. He became Beethoven's patron and most probably invited him to play at his home shortly after their acquaintance had begun. Beethoven became a talking point in the aristocratic society into which he had been admitted on the recommendation of his patrons at Bonn, though his rough manner was only tolerated because he was so very highly admired as a musician.

In the 1790s the nearest equivalent to the piano recital of today took place in the drawing rooms of aristocratic households. Whereas the pianist today can expect a respectful silence, at least when he starts his programme of chosen pieces, the pianist of Beethoven's day certainly could not. He had to wait to be asked by his host, during the polite conversation, if he would care to entertain the company by playing. Perhaps the most popular form of entertainment at these musical parties was the competitive display of extemporization at the piano. Instead of performing music which was already familiar, each pianist improvised either on his own material or on a theme which someone in the party might have given him. If the improvisation was boring people did not feel restrained from talking, moving around or even going out. When Beethoven entered this circle, far from behaving like a Rhineland provincial impressed by the sophistication of the Austrian capital city, he had the force of character to make people realize that *he was insisting* on getting respect from them. If he was going to play, his audience had to give him their attention, princes, barons, everybody. He'd refuse to begin until people stopped talking. This was audacity his aristocratic audience had not met with before. It was startling, but worth condoning because he was such an extraordinarily good musician.

His improvisations were quite unlike anyone else's. His character came through forcibly in the music, conveyed by means of a virtuoso technique. His reputation grew as, inevitably, rumours circulated about piano 'duels' he had won against other pianists who played in Vienna: how his improvisation, at such-and-such a soirée had eclipsed that of a rival virtuoso present to such an extent that the other had refused ever since to play at any party to which Beethoven had been invited. And he became known internationally after his tours in 1796 to Berlin, Prague, Leipzig and Budapest.

In a letter to Breitkopf & Härtel, the music publishers in Leipzig, in December 1802, Beethoven makes a clear distinction between his major works and the others, recognizing the major ones by the award of an opus number. His *Nine variations for piano* had been published when he was twelve, and since then he had amassed a pile of his scores, which he had taken with him to Vienna. It was important to him that he should make a favourable impression on his aristocratic admirers who knew him as the great improviser who had written the

Figure 5 Soirée in the palace of Moritz von Fries in Vienna, drawing by J. Fischer, 1800 (Historisches Museum of the City of Vienna. The original disappeared in 1945; from a photograph in the possession of H. C. Robbins Landon).

concerto he had played at the charity concert. Beethoven was not willing to let his future as a composer be gauged on the merits of this concerto in B flat: he was not going to have that *published* as his first work in Vienna, he had other far better things, and was under no misapprehension as to the concerto's worth. He kept it back, in fact, until he had established his reputation as a composer, then offered it to Hoffmeister on the cheap, 'I am valuing the concerto at only 10 ducats because, as I have already told you, I do not consider it to be one of my best concertos'. It was published in 1801. The composition he selected for his op. 1 and op. 2 publications must be amongst the most confident and powerful ever to appear under such low opus numbers.[1]

The op. 1 is a set of three piano trios and the op. 2 his first set of sonatas for piano solo. His own instrument thus created the impact he was hoping for. The piano-violin-cello combination was already popular, one which Beethoven had experience of playing and could handle with mastery by now – he had already written two piano trios before starting on the op. 1 set, but these again he held back, and when eventually they were published neither of them received an opus number. He composed the three piano trios of the op. 1 set while he was supposed to be under Haydn's supervision, and it happens that Haydn was at that time also writing piano trios with great fluency. Beethoven's first three were published in 1795 – and about that time Haydn published ten. It was when Haydn heard the third of Beethoven's piano trios that he aroused the younger man's antagonism. The three are strong works in Beethoven's confident and disturbing style. Haydn thought the third was far too disturbing and that to publish it might prejudice Beethoven's chances of success.

EXERCISE

Read the account on pages 48 and 49 of *Beethoven, Impressions by his Contemporaries*, then make a note of your answers to the questions based on this passage. In this and all the exercises which follow, do attempt *all* the questions in the exercise before referring to the answers.

1 What two things do you learn about Haydn from this account?

---

[1]A movement from *Piano Sonata in C major, op. 2 no. 3* is included on the SECOND BEETHOVEN RECORD.

2　How important did Beethoven consider Haydn's supervision?

3　Beethoven misconstrued Haydn's criticism. Why did he think Haydn advised him not to publish the C minor trio?

4　On what grounds did Haydn advise him in this way?

Do this before going on

SPECIMEN ANSWERS

1　It shows that Haydn was very highly regarded in Vienna, and that his verdict counted a lot. Knowing his public well, he advised Beethoven not to risk a failure with a composition which might not be understood. You might have put this less kindly and said that Haydn was conservative and concerned only with pleasing the public with the old familiar kind of music.

2　He clearly didn't consider it important as there hadn't been any supervision at all, this performance at Prince Lichnowsky's soirée being the first time Haydn heard the trios.

3　Because he thought Haydn was envious and unwilling to help him.

4　See the last sentence in the paragraph. Further, if Haydn really thought there was a danger of the C minor trio not succeeding with the public, and had *not* advised Beethoven as he did, he could be suspected of malice.

Of the three piano trios, the third in C minor bears most strongly the stamp of its composer's personality, in its powerful rhythms and the urgent inevitability of movement; yet although these are the very qualities that appeal to us now it was their novelty which caused Haydn apprehension. The set of three piano trios was published in 1795, dedicated to Prince Lichnowsky.

The element of virtuosity seen in the piano writing of the trios reaches a higher degree in the solo writing of the op. 2 piano sonatas. Here is writing of a brilliant kind. Beethoven the man was confident and forceful, so is the music of this period; it demands your attention as Beethoven demanded attention of those who listened to him perform. The three sonatas for piano, op. 2, dedicated to Haydn, were published in March 1796.

Beethoven lived in the age of Mozart and Haydn, and used their musical language as his raw material in such a way that it became his own, and bore the pecularities of his own style strongly upon it. This he was well aware of, and the healthy conceit he had may be seen in the following postscript to a letter he wrote to Eleonore von Breuning of Bonn, in the early summer of 1794.

> The variations will be rather difficult to play, and particularly the trills in the coda. But this must not intimidate and discourage you. For the composition is so arranged that you need only play the trill and can leave out the other notes, since these appear in the violin part as well. I should never have written down this kind of piece, had I not already noticed fairly often how some people in Vienna after hearing me extemporize of an evening would note down on the following day several peculiarities of my style and palm them off with pride as their own. Well, as I foresaw that their pieces would soon be published, I resolved to forestall those people. But there was yet another reason, namely my desire to embarrass those Viennese pianists, some of whom are my sworn enemies. I wanted to revenge myself on them in this way, because I knew beforehand that my variations would here and there be put before the said gentlemen and that they would cut a sorry figure with them.
>
> (*Selected letters of Beethoven*, p. 12.)

The work in question, incidentally, was the *Twelve variations for violin and piano on Mozart's 'Se vuol ballare'*[1]. Opera lovers may know the latter, in one of the

---

[1]Beethoven did not ascribe an opus number to it, but recently in Georg Kinsky, *Das Werk Beethovens. Thematisch-bibliographisches Verzeichnis seiner sämtlichen vollendeten Kompositionen*, Munich, 1955, compositions without opus numbers were given a means of identification and this one is WoO 40 – i.e. *Werke ohne Opuszahl* 'works without an opus number', number 40.

English translations, as 'If you are after a little amusement', one of Figaro's arias in the first act of Mozart's enormously entertaining comic opera *The Marriage of Figaro*. The Viennese public had given the opera a luke-warm reception on its first appearance in May 1786, but it was produced at Prague that December with unprecedented success. Mozart accepted an invitation to Prague, arriving 11 January 1787, and was able to write to a friend, 'people here talk of nothing but *Figaro* . . . It is certainly a feather in my cap'. The opera was given repeatedly to full houses; many of the big tunes were published in dance arrangements under the title 'German dances of 1787', and the melody of the aria in question, 'Se vuol ballare', even found its way into a school songbook written in 1787 to words of a 'spring song'![1] Taking its cue from Prague, Vienna gave *Figaro* an enthusiastic reception in subsequent performances (social and political reasons undoubtedly playing a part) and it has since become one of the most popular of all operas. Only two months after Mozart's return from Prague, he is said to have met the sixteen-year-old Beethoven on his first, short visit to Vienna. If Beethoven was not then aware of the success of *Figaro* it is impossible for him not to have heard about it after returning to settle there; hence this set of variations on an aria of Figaro's in response to the public's liking for it and for the way he improvised on the melody. But as usual, Beethoven had no pretensions about its worth: it is a pretty drawing-room piece, no more. He sent a copy of it to Eleonore saying, 'I thought that these trifles might possibly afford you some pleasure'. Trifles like this do often give pleasure to player and listener alike but it is a different kind from that afforded by Beethoven's seriously considered compositions.

In his op. 1 and op. 2 publications Beethoven presented the Viennese aristocracy with convincing evidence of his stature as a composer. In tracing his development as an artist we might observe that their publication when he was twenty-four and twenty-five years of age indicate the time he reached success as a composer. He was also considered the finest of virtuoso pianists. It is of interest too that he did not work as a church musician or play in an orchestra for his living, but was independent, in fact was one of the first outstanding free-lance musicians.

EXERCISE

Beethoven's Professionalism

Basing your answer on your reading so far in these units write notes referring to specific points of Beethoven's conduct as a professional musician. To get the complete picture you should include his conduct as a businessman. In my answer, I give ten points. Perhaps you can think of more.

Do this before going on

SPECIMEN ANSWERS

Here are the points which occur to me.

1 He was a superb performer and quite exceptional as an improviser.
2 He had started as a musician at court but was now working free-lance. Probably this was by choice, but to some extent it was the outcome of circumstances beyond his control, in that he couldn't return to the post he'd had at Bonn.
3 He knew the value of his own style and wanted to have the benefit of selling it, and not seeing it passed off as his rivals.

[1]Erich Schenk, *Mozart and his Times*, London, Secker and Warburg, 1960, pp. 378–84.

4   Hence, the tricky pieces with which he hoped to disgrace his rivals.

5   He wrote *salon* pieces as well as his more seriously considered compositions, because he performed them himself and stood to gain on account of the popularity of that kind of music.

6   He was well aware of the musical value of his work, denoting his major works only with opus numbers.

7   He kept back his poorer, often earlier, compositions until he had established himself as a composer and then, when he considered 'inferior works' couldn't do his reputation any harm, sold them cheaply (or perhaps, for as much as he dared ask!).

8   He was singularly independent. He asserted his individuality both in his playing and the style of his compositions.

9   Though his excitable, abrasive manner was no commercial affectation, it nevertheless made him a talking-point in Viennese high society, with the consequence that his professional services as a performer were the more in demand.

10   He was daring, perhaps truer to say reckless, and he cared little for convention for its own sake.

That Beethoven was known to the nobility and aristocracy of the Austro-Hungarian Empire is shown by the very impressive list of subscribers to his op. 1 piano trios. With only one or two exceptions, every subscriber is of the rank of either a prince, a count, a baron or a lord.

In the five years between the publication of his op. 1 piano trios and the turn of the century, Beethoven was mainly occupied with composition, although he was on tour as a performer in 1796 and again in 1798. The publications that had established his reputation were followed by a number of works in which Beethoven's own instrument, the piano, was almost invariably involved: more piano sonatas (including his op. 13 the *Pathétique*); sets of variations; another piano trio; a quintet for oboe, clarinet, bassoon, horn and piano; various songs with orchestral or piano accompaniment; three trios and a serenade for violin, viola and cello; other pieces of chamber music for strings and wind instruments; and a piano concerto (no. 1 in C major, op. 15, was written *after* the concerto mentioned already, known as no. 2 in B flat, which Beethoven chose to revise before its publication).

At this time he was famous as the great performer not as a composer, and as he was later to write in a letter (see page 19), he might have had a profitable career travelling around Europe as a virtuoso pianist had it not been for what he certainly viewed with dismay for a time, and what might have been disastrous for him as a musician: the onset of deafness.

Traditionally Beethoven's output has been divided into the works of three periods, a division, as his friend and first biographer, Anton Schindler (1795–1864), pointed out, arising not 'out of the history of the development of his genius, but purely from the various phases of his life, such as Beethoven himself would have adopted'. (*The Life of Beethoven*, trans. and ed. Ignace Moscheles (1841), Mattapan, Mass., Gamut Music Company, 1966, p. 14.)

One cannot divorce life and genius, and it should be emphasized that these periods are related *in a general way* to his age and maturity, and to the state of his hearing. Compositions of his 'early period' were written when he was young, when he could hear and was able to perform as a solo pianist. This means up to *about* 1800. The 'middle period' takes in the works between then and 1815, and the 'late period' extended up to his death in 1827. During the middle and late periods he was able to hear progressively less; some days it seems his hearing was better than others but on the whole by 1815 he could usually hear very little indeed, and finally he could not hear anything. With his hearing deteriorating he was not able to perform in public as a pianist, nor could he give piano lessons as he had done nor conduct an orchestra effectively. These are guide-lines, and where to make the distinction between the early and middle periods can only be tentatively suggested. The date 1800–1 is taken because, as we shall shortly be discussing, at this time there occurred a *change of spirit* in his music.

Beethoven did on rare occasions continue to perform publicly to the end of the middle period, though with unfortunate if not always catastrophic results. The German composer and violinist, Louis Spohr, heard him in 1814 at a rehearsal for the first public performance of the piano trio op. 97, known as the *Archduke* trio. He wrote:

> It was by no means an enjoyment; for in the first place the piano was woefully out of tune which, however, troubled Beethoven little, since he could hear nothing of it and, secondly, of the former so admired excellence of the virtuoso scarcely anything was left, in consequence of his total deafness. In the *forte*, the poor deaf man hammered in such a way upon the keys that entire groups of notes were inaudible, so that one lost all intelligence of the subject unless the eye followed the score at the same time.

Look up Spohr's very readable report of his encounter with Beethoven, in the set book, *Beethoven, Impressions by his Contemporaries*, pages 94–100.

Do this before going on

There was a break in his output between the middle and late periods but here again, while the dates of publication might seem to confirm a clear division, characteristics in the style of the late period may already be seen in music dating from before the break in continuity. Remember then, that in referring to music of a certain *period* I am doing so well aware of the limitations and the value of such designation. And that while it is, perhaps, more interesting to note what was *new* in the works of each period, to get the whole picture we should remember that there was also a continuing development, even right from his earliest works.

In many respects the music of the early period resembles that of Mozart and Haydn in style. As noted above, certain characteristics are already present, later to be emphasized, which distinguish the music as Beethoven's, yet, to take two compositions I have referred to earlier – the op. 19 piano concerto and the violin and piano variations on Mozart's 'Se vuol ballare' – these are similar in style and scope to very many compositions in the musical language of the late eighteenth century. Beethoven's op. 1 piano trios and op. 2 solo sonatas, with which he deliberately set out to make an impact on his public *as a composer*, are similar again in style even if they are marked, as the works cited above are not, by an overt seriousness of purpose which we recognize as a distinguishing, personal characteristic of Beethoven's.

His was an age of revolutions, and Beethoven was a child of his time. He believed in the individual, in his stand against subordination and convention. He was strongly influenced by both the ideas and the turn of events in the French revolutions. And he certainly had a high opinion of Napoleon. Alive at the same time as Mozart and Haydn, Beethoven was not of their generations. In the 1790s he was a man of the *modern* world in which he worked. This is what marked him out from them. Ultimately, when we try to define the differences between his music and theirs, and have drawn attention to details of technique, we have to resort to something which is more easily felt than illustrated: we say that the *spirit* of his music is different from theirs. He was not a servant at any court after settling in Vienna, and in 1809 he turned down a post at Kassel as *Kapellmeister* to the King of Westphalia. He did not want to compose court music but music *for everyone* who would listen to him (and perhaps with a tinge of materialism he would have said, 'the more the better!'). With regard to his publishers, the public and his private patrons, his behaviour was unusual. But how he personified the revolutionary spirit of his age was something more than this singular independence of manner: there are reverberations in his music of his own very real struggle to come to grips with a way of life forced on him by deafness, the consequences of which dismayed him.

When Beethoven began to notice that he was getting hard of hearing he was a young man of twenty-eight and his reaction was naturally optimistic, he felt sure he would get over it. When it appeared not to be getting any better he began to be seriously disturbed. The prospect of deafness as he approached thirty was alarming in the extreme. To observe when it was that the change in *the spirit* of his music came about, and possibly to appreciate why it happened, we should consider how Beethoven faced up to this emotional crisis.

He kept the secret of his increasing deafness for about two or three years before confiding, by letter, in his friends Amenda and Wegeler. Karl Amenda (1771–1836) and Beethoven became close friends when in 1798 Amenda had come to Vienna as tutor to the children of one of Beethoven's patrons, Prince Lobkowitz. Amenda stayed about a year and afterwards he and Beethoven kept in touch. Franz Gerhard Wegeler (1765–1848) had been a friend at the von Breuning household at Bonn, and in fact he was later to marry Beethoven's friend

Eleonore.[1] He had a distinguished career as a medical consultant, hence the amount of detail Beethoven goes into, describing his illness in the letters from which the following extracts are taken. Besides the letters to Wegeler and Amenda in 1801, there is one other important document in which Beethoven, in a state of extreme depression describes the crisis he was in. It is written as a sort of will addressed to his brothers (but never sent), in terms indicating that he thought he was soon to die. *The Heiligenstadt Testament*, and the footnote he added four days later, is given in full. It takes its name from the village where it was written, one of the places out in the country to which Beethoven resorted during the hot summer months.

He contradicts himself often enough, but *what do you think* are the points which Beethoven seems to be emphasizing? When you have found these points, do you understand him any better? I'll be suggesting what you might look for in the exercise which follows. Meanwhile, read the extracts with a mind for the implications which permanent deafness had for a musician of Beethoven's temperament and standing.

To Franz Gerhard Wegeler, Bonn.

Vienna, 29 June 1801

My dear, kind Wegeler,

I do thank you most warmly for your remembrance of me which I have so little deserved or even endeavoured to deserve where you are concerned . . .

There are moments when I myself long for you and, what is more, would like to spend some time with you – For my Fatherland, the beautiful country where I first opened my eyes to the light, still seems to me as lovely and as clearly before my eyes as it was when I left you. In short, the day on which I can meet you again and greet our Father Rhine I shall regard as one of the happiest of my life – When that will be I cannot yet tell you. But indeed I can assure you that when we meet you will certainly see that I have become a first-rate fellow; not only as an artist but also as a man you will find me better and more fully developed. And if our Fatherland is then in a more prosperous condition, my art will be exercised only for the benefit of the poor. Oh blissful moment, how happy do I count myself that I can help to produce you, that I myself can create you – You want to know something about my present situation. Well, on the whole it is not at all bad. For since last year Lichnowsky . . . has disbursed for my benefit a fixed sum of 600 gulden, on which I can draw until I obtain a suitable appointment. My compositions bring me in a good deal; and I may say that I am offered more commissions than it is possible for me to carry out. Moreover for every composition I can count on six or seven publishers, and even more, if I want them; people no longer come to an arrangement with me, I state my price and they pay. So you see how pleasantly situated I am . . .

Moreover, I live more economically than I used to; and if I remain in Vienna for good, no doubt I shall contrive to obtain one day for a concert every year. I have given a few concerts. But that jealous demon, my wretched health, has put a nasty spoke in my wheel; and it amounts to this, that for the last three years my hearing has become weaker and weaker. The trouble is supposed to have been caused by the condition of my abdomen which, as you know, was wretched even before I left Bonn, but has become worse in Vienna . . .

Such was my condition until the autumn of last year; and sometimes I gave way to despair . . .

My deafness persisted or, I should say, became even worse . . .

my ears continue to hum and buzz day and night. I must confess that I lead a miserable life. For almost two years I have ceased to attend any social functions, just because I find it impossible to say to people: I am deaf. If I had any other profession I might be able to cope with my infirmity; but in my profession it is a terrible handicap. And if my enemies, of whom I have a fair number, were to hear about it, what would they say? –

[1]For these biographical details and the full text of the documents quoted overleaf see *Selected letters of Beethoven*, pp. 16, 31–42.

In order to give you some idea of this strange deafness, let me tell you that in the theatre I have to place myself quite close to the orchestra in order to understand what the actor is saying, and that at a distance I cannot hear the high notes of instruments or voices. As for the spoken voice it is surprising that some people have never noticed my deafness; but since I have always been liable to fits of absentmindedness, they attribute my hardness of hearing to that. Sometimes too I can scarcely hear a person who speaks softly; I can hear sounds, it is true, but cannot make out the words. But if anyone shouts I can't bear it. Heaven alone knows what is to become of me . . .

Already I have often cursed my Creator and my existence. Plutarch has shown me *the path of resignation*. If it is at all possible, I will bid defiance to my fate, though I feel that as long as I live there will be moments when I shall be God's most unhappy creature – I beg you not to say anything about my condition to any one . . .

I am only telling you this as a secret . . .

If my trouble persists, I will visit you next spring. You will rent a house for me in some beautiful part of the country and then for six months I will lead the life of a peasant. Perhaps that will make a difference. Resignation, what a wretched resource! Yet it is all that is left to me . . .

Frankly, your love of art still gives me the greatest pleasure. If you let me know how to set about it, I will send you all my works, which, I must admit, now amount to quite a fair number, a number which is daily increasing . . .

I live entirely in my music; and hardly have I completed one composition when I have already begun another. At my present rate of composing, I often produce three or four works at the same time – Now do write to me more often and I will make a point of finding time to write to you occasionally . . .

As for Ries, to whom I send cordial greetings, I will write to you more fully about his son, although I think that he could make his fortune more easily in *Paris* than in *Vienna*. Vienna is flooded with musicians and thus even the most deserving find it difficult to make a living – But in the autumn or the winter when people are hurrying back to town I will see what I can do for him – All good wishes, kind and faithful Wegeler; and rest assured of the affection and friendship of your

BEETHOVEN.

To Karl Amenda, Mirben, Near Talsen, Courland.

Vienna, 1 July [1801]

My dear Amenda, my kind Amenda, my warm-hearted Friend!

I received and read your last letter with intense emotion and with mixed feelings of pain and pleasure – To what shall I compare your loyalty to me, your affection for me? Oh, how splendid it is that you have remained so constant to me; and indeed I know that you more than all the others have proved your friendship for me and that you deserve to be my chosen friend. You are no *Viennese friend*, no, you are one of those such as my native soil is wont to produce. How often would I like to have you here with me, for your Beethoven is leading a very unhappy life and is at variance with Nature and his Creator. Many times already I have cursed Him for exposing His creatures to the slightest hazard, so that the most beautiful blossom is thereby often crushed and destroyed. Let me tell you that my most prized possession, *my hearing*, has greatly deteriorated. When you were still with me, I already felt the symptoms; but I said nothing about them. Now they have become very much worse. We must wait and see whether my hearing can be restored. The symptoms are said to be caused by the condition of my abdomen. So far as the latter is concerned, I am almost quite cured. But that my hearing too will improve, I must hope, it is true, but I hardly think it possible, for diseases of that kind are the most difficult to cure. You will realize what a sad life I must now lead, seeing that I am cut off from everything that is dear and precious to me and, what is more, I have to associate with such miserable egoists . . . I may say that of all of them Lichnowsky has best stood the test. During this last year he has disbursed for my benefit 600 gulden. This sum and the steady sale of my works enable me to live without financial anxiety. Everything I compose now can be sold immediately five times over and be well paid for too – Meanwhile I have been composing a good deal . . .

Oh how happy should I be now if I had perfect hearing, for then I would join you immediately. But in my present condition I must withdraw from everything; and my best years will rapidly pass away without my being able to achieve all that my talent and my strength have commanded me to do – Sad resignation, to which I am forced to have recourse. Needless to say, I am resolved to overcome all this, but how is it going to be done? Yes, Amenda, if after six months my disease proves to be incurable, then I shall claim your sympathy, then you must give up everything and come to me. I shall then travel (when I am playing and composing, my affliction still hampers me least; it affects me most when I am in company) and you must be my companion. I am convinced that my luck will not forsake me. Why, at the moment I feel equal to anything. Since your departure I have been composing all types of music, except operas and sacred works. I feel sure you will not refuse my request; I know that you will help your friend to bear his troubles and his infirmity. My pianoforte playing too has considerably improved; and I hope that our tour will perhaps enable you to make your fortune as well; and then you will stay with me for ever – I have safely received all your letters. Although I have replied to them so seldom, yet you have always been present in my thoughts; and my heart beats just as tenderly for you as ever – *I beg you to treat what I have told you about my hearing as a great secret to be entrusted to no one, whoever he may be* – Write to me very often, for your letters, however short they may be, console me and do me good. Hence I shall expect another letter from you soon my dear fellow . . .

your faithful, your truly devoted

L. V. BEETHOVEN

To Franz Gerhard Wegeler, Bonn.

Vienna, 16 November [1801]

My dear, kind Wegeler!

I thank you for this fresh proof of your anxiety about me, the more so as I deserve it so little where you are concerned . . . the humming and buzzing is slightly less than it used to be, particularly in my left ear, where my deafness really began. But so far my hearing is certainly not a bit better; and I am inclined to think, although I do not dare to say so definitely, that it is a little weaker . . .

I am now leading a slightly more pleasant life, for I am mixing more with my fellow creatures. You would find it hard to believe what an empty, sad life I have had for the last two years. My poor hearing haunted me everywhere like a ghost; and I avoided – all human society. I seemed to be a misanthrope and yet am far from being one. This change has been brought about by a dear charming girl who loves me and whom I love. After two years I am again enjoying a few blissful moments; and for the first time I feel that – marriage might bring me happiness. Unfortunately she is not of my class – and at the moment – I certainly could not marry – I must still bustle about a good deal. Had it not been for my deafness, I should have long ago travelled half the world over; and that I must do – For to me there is no greater pleasure than to practise and exercise my art – Do not imagine that I should be happy living with you at Bonn. In any case what is there to make me any happier? Even your anxiety would hurt me. Every moment I should see your face expressing pity and should only feel more unhappy – Those beautiful parts of my native land, what did they give me but the hope of bettering my circumstances? And this I should have done – but for my present affliction – Oh, if only I could be rid of it I would embrace the whole world – My youth, yes, I feel it, is only just beginning, for was I not always a sickly fellow? For some time now my physical strength has been increasing more and more, and therefore my mental powers also. Every day brings me nearer to the goal which I feel but cannot describe. And it is only in that condition that your Beethoven can live. There must be no rest – I know of none but sleep, and indeed I am heartily sorry that I must now give more time to sleep than I used to do. If only I can be partially liberated from my affliction, then – I will come to you as a complete and mature man, and renew our old feelings of friendship. You will find me as happy as I am fated to be on this earth, not unhappy – no, that I could not bear – I will seize Fate by the throat; it shall certainly not bend and crush me completely – Oh, it would be so lovely to live a thousand lives – No indeed, I realize now that I am no longer suited to a quiet life – Do write to me as soon as possible – . . .

BTHVN.

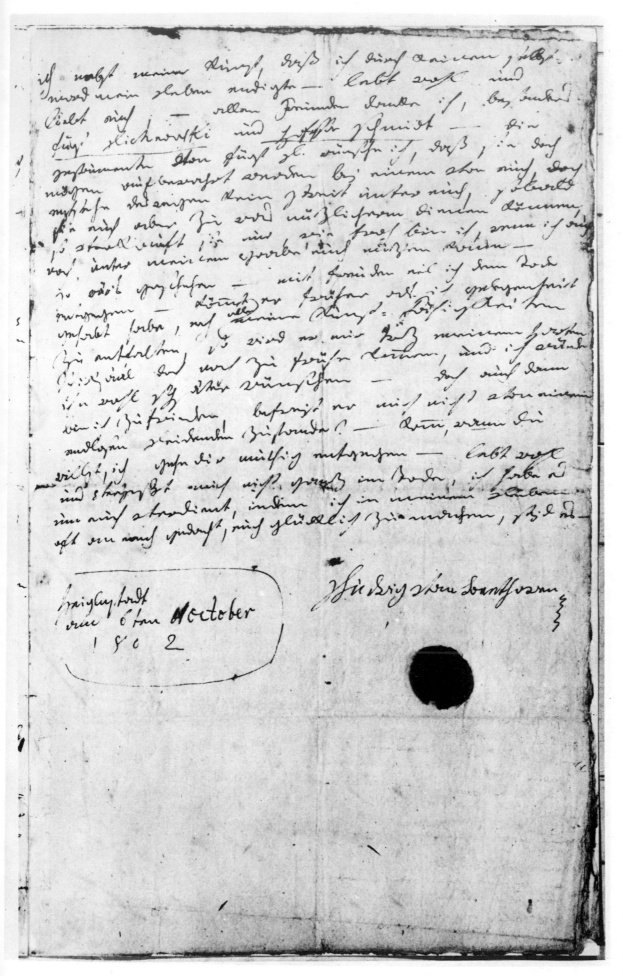

Figure 7 End of 'Heiligenstadt Testament' (6 October 1802) (Staats- und Universitätsbibliothek, Hamburg).

20

To Caspar Anton Carl and [Nikolaus Johann][1] van Beethoven.

Heiligenstadt, 6 October 1802.

For my Brothers Carl and [Johann] Beethoven

O my fellow men, who consider me, or describe me as, unfriendly, peevish or even misanthropic, how greatly do you wrong me. For you do not know the secret reason why I appear to you to be so. Ever since my childhood my heart and soul have been imbued with the tender feeling of goodwill; and I have always been ready to perform even great actions. But just think, for the last six years I have been afflicted with an incurable complaint which has been made worse by incompetent doctors. From year to year my hopes of being cured have gradually been shattered and finally I have been forced to accept the prospect of a *permanent infirmity* (the curing of which may perhaps take years or may even prove to be impossible). Though endowed with a passionate and lively temperament and even fond of the distractions offered by society I was soon obliged to seclude myself and live in solitude. If at times I decided just to ignore my infirmity, alas! how cruelly was I then driven back by the intensified sad experience of my poor hearing. Yet I could not bring myself to say to people: 'Speak up, shout, for I am deaf'. Alas! how could I possibly refer to the impairing *of a sense* which in me should be more perfectly developed than in other people, a sense which at one time I possessed in the greatest perfection, even to a degree of perfection such as assuredly few in my profession possess or have ever possessed – Oh, I cannot do it; so forgive me, if you ever see me withdrawing from your company which I used to enjoy. Moreover my misfortune pains me doubly, inasmuch as it leads to my being misjudged. For me there can be no relaxation in human society, no refined conversations, no mutual confidences. I must live quite alone and may creep into society only as often as sheer necessity demands; I must live like an outcast. If I appear in company I am overcome by a burning anxiety, a fear that I am running the risk of letting people notice my condition – And that has been my experience during the last six months which I have spent in the country. My sensible doctor by suggesting that I should spare my hearing as much as possible has more or less encouraged my present and natural inclination, though indeed when carried away now and then by my instinctive desire for human society, I have let myself be tempted to seek it. But how humiliated I have felt if somebody standing beside me heard the sound of a flute in the distance and *I heard nothing*, or if somebody heard *a shepherd sing* and again I heard nothing – Such experiences almost made me despair, and I was on the point of putting an end to my life – The only thing that held me back was *my art*. For indeed it seemed to me impossible to leave this world before I had produced all the works that I felt the urge to compose; and thus I have dragged on this miserable existence – a truly miserable existence, seeing that I have such a sensitive body that any fairly sudden change can plunge me from the best spirits into the worst of humours – *Patience* – that is the virtue, I am told, which I must now choose for my guide; and I now possess it – I hope that I shall persist in my resolve to endure to the end, until it pleases the inexorable Parcae to cut the thread; perhaps my condition will improve, perhaps not; at any rate I am resigned – At the early age of 28 I was obliged to become a philosopher, though this was not easy; for indeed this is more difficult for an artist than for anyone else – Almighty God, who looks down into my innermost soul, you see into my heart and you know that it is filled with love for humanity and a desire to do good. Oh my fellow men, when some day you read this statement, remember that you have done me wrong; and let some unfortunate man derive comfort from the thought that he has found another equally unfortunate who, notwithstanding all the obstacles imposed by nature, yet did everything in his power to be raised to the rank of noble artists and human beings – And you, my brothers Carl and [Johann], when I am dead, request on my behalf Professor Schmidt, if he is still living, to describe my disease, and attach this written document to his record, so that after my death at any rate the world and I may be reconciled as far a possible – At the same time I herewith nominate you both heirs to my small property (if I may so describe it) – Divide it honestly, live in harmony and help one another. You know that you have long ago been forgiven for the harm you did me. I again thank you, my brother Carl, in particular, for the affection you have shown me of late years. My wish is that you should have a better and more carefree existence than I have had. Urge your children to be *virtuous*, for virtue alone can make a man happy. Money cannot do this. I speak from experience. It was virtue that sustained me in my misery. It was thanks to virtue and also to my art that I did not put an end to my life by suicide –

---

[1]This brother was known as 'Nikolaus' in childhood but 'Johann' in later years. Possibly Beethoven was uncertain which name to use in something like a legal document, so he left a blank wherever the name was needed.

Farewell and love one another – I thank all my friends, and especially *Prince Lichnowsky* and *Professor Schmidt*. I would like Prince Lichnowsky's instruments to be preserved by one of you, provided this does not lead to a quarrel between you. But as soon as they can serve a more useful purpose, just sell them; and how glad I shall be if in my grave I can still be of some use to you both – Well, that is all – Joyfully I go to meet Death – should it come before I have had an opportunity of developing all my artistic gifts, then in spite of my hard fate it would still come too soon, and no doubt I would like it to postpone its coming – Yet even so I should be content, for would it not free me from a condition of continual suffering? Come then, Death, *whenever* you like, and with courage I will go to meet you – Farewell; and when I am dead, do not wholly forget me. I deserve to be remembered by you, since during my lifetime I have often thought of you and tried to make you happy – Be happy –

LUDWIG VAN BEETHOVEN.

For my brothers Carl and [Johann]
To be read and executed after my death –
Heiligenstadt, 10 October 1802.

Thus I take leave of you – and, what is more, rather sadly – yes, the hope I cherished – the hope I brought with me here of being cured to a certain extent at any rate – that hope I must now abandon completely. As the autumn leaves fall and wither, likewise – that hope has faded for me. I am leaving here – almost in the same condition as I arrived – Even that high courage – which has often inspired me on fine summer days – has vanished – Oh Providence – do but grant me one day *of pure joy* – For so long now the inner echo of real joy has been unknown to me – Oh when – oh, when, Almighty God – shall I be able to hear and feel this echo again in the temple of Nature and in contact with humanity – Never? – No! – Oh, that would be too hard.

(The above extracts are from *Selected letters of Beethoven*, pp. 31–42, 258–61.)

EXERCISE

1 What does Beethoven think is the cause of his disability?
2 What outcome of his deafness seems to cause him most distress?
3 What do you gather about his feelings for the Viennese?
4 How optimistic does he appear to be about a cure?
5 What does he think of doing as a cure, if his disability persists?
6 He makes some rather astonishing comments about his professional activities. What are they?
7 Beethoven mentions three quite different means of gaining release from his predicament. What are these three possibilities?

Do this before going on

SPECIMEN ANSWERS[1]

1 An abdominal complaint: both this and his hearing having been made worse by incompetent doctors.
2 He is greatly distressed at being forced out of society, which he enjoys. Although he also likes being alone, he doesn't care for *such* a degree of isolation. His pride, and also very real fear, prevents him telling anybody that he is deaf, and when he doesn't catch something he allows people to attribute his odd behaviour to fits of absent-mindedness. Particularly, he is concerned about his profession (see p. 21) and is anxious that his enemies won't get to know.
3 He obviously harbours a grudge against them, because, 'I must live quite alone . . . like an outcast'. His heart is full of tender feelings of goodwill and he is being misjudged, described as 'peevish or even misanthropic' – which he is not.
4 Not very. Even in 1801 he had little hope for his hearing although his abdominal troubles were better and his strength was increasing. In the

[1] I am indebted to Alan Tyson's article 'Beethoven's heroic phase', *The Musical Times*, February 1969, pp. 139–41. If you care to look further into this see also Tyson, 'An Angry letter for Beethoven', *The Musical Times*, September 1971.

Figure 8 Quartet of instruments presented to Beethoven by Prince Carl Lichnowsky 1800, with Beethoven's own viola. From left to right: viola (V. Rugero 1690); cello (A. Guarnerius 1675); viola (maker unknown) violins by (N. Amati 1690 and G. Guarnerius 1718).

Heiligenstadt Testament the following year, he recognizes 'the prospect of a *permanent infirmity*'.

5   He will either go to live in the country, leading the life of a peasant for six months or travel – both possibilities taking him away from Vienna.

6   He is least hampered when he is playing and composing. He seems to be in good form, composing a great deal (and is happy to have the music publishers offering high prices), in fact 'all types of music, except operas and sacred works'. His piano playing has improved, and he momentarily thinks of going on tour. Every day brings him nearer to the goal which he can feel but cannot describe.

7   (a)   Through love for 'a dear charming girl', who gives him the hope that his disability might be forgotten in the happiness achieved in marriage.
   (b)   The easy way out: 'Come then, Death, *whenever* you like.'
   (c)   The heroic stand: 'I will seize Fate by the throat; it shall certainly not bend and crush me completely.' He will triumph through his music.

DISCUSSION

When a musician loses his hearing he is deprived of the medium in which he is a specialist. Beethoven used to call himself a *Tondichter*, a poet or artist in sound. At that early stage, in 1801, Beethoven's distress about his deafness was occasioned more by the fact that it was a social liability than because it limited his activities as a musician. In the course of training, musicians learn to hear music *mentally*, and with experience may be able to imagine accurately how a score would sound if it were played by the forces specified. Beethoven had a fine mental ear, i.e. what he heard mentally must have resembled a live performance very closely. Not being able to hear aurally while he was composing consequently wasn't much of a drawback to him. When he was playing or composing, he writes to Amenda, he was least aware of his disability. I think it is interesting to note how much pain his professional fear inflicts on him: he finds it *impossible to say* to people he is deaf, and allows them to attribute odd behaviour on his part to fits of absent-mindedness; he implores Wegeler and Amenda not to tell anybody about it, he is particularly afraid of his enemies getting to know that this sense is impaired which, 'at one time I possessed in the greatest perfection, even to a degree of perfection such as assuredly few in my profession possess or have ever possessed.' The second letter to Wegeler shows that even though his hearing has perhaps become even weaker he has come to a happier relationship with society: 'I am now leading a slightly more pleasant life, for I am mixing more with my fellow creatures.' He has been induced back through love for 'a dear charming girl', probably the seventeen-year-old Countess Giulietta Guicciardi, who had given him confidence to believe that marriage might bring him happiness. With delightful nonchalance – 'Unfortunately she is not of my class' – he hastens to avoid this delicate issue, mentioning the work and playing to be done when he gets better.

Beethoven was preoccupied with the thought of permanent deafness, but he continued composing with complete dedication. From the turn of the century he wrote fewer compositions each year, but the scale of his works became larger. With his first two symphonies,[1] his first set of six string quartets and a string quintet, Beethoven was writing in what were for him new media and was tending away from the piano-orientated kind of works which had mainly occupied him before. He certainly did not, however, *stop* writing from then on for the piano. He was still to compose another three piano concertos, solo sonatas up to a total of thirty-two and many other miscellaneous pieces. And in the year 1801 he composed possibly the most well known of his piano pieces today: the sonata op. 27 no. 2, nicknamed the *Moonlight* sonata. That he was consciously trying out new media may be taken from the letter to Amenda, which you have already studied, 'Since your departure I have been composing all types of music, except operas and sacred works'.

Furthermore, *he felt* that his music was changing and indeed had changed. We can see this for instance in the apologetic letter he wrote in 1800 to the poet Friedrich von Matthisson (1761–1831), informing him rather belatedly that he had dedicated his own setting of Matthisson's *Adelaide* to him. The song was written back in 1795 or '96. By 1800 Beethoven, who was requesting another of his poems to set, knew he had changed his style and didn't want the poet to think that what he wrote then would be like what he had written before, 'You yourself are aware what changes a few years may produce in an artist who is constantly progressing. The greater the strides he makes in his art, the less is he satisfied with his earlier works' (*Selected letters of Beethoven*, p. 22). And the pianist Carl Czerny (1791–1857) quotes Beethoven as having told a close friend about this time, 'I am not very well satisfied with the work I have thus far done. From this day on I shall take a new way.' (You might look this up: it is on page 31 of *Beethoven, Impressions by his Contemporaries*.)

Do this before going on

I admit that I am doubtful about the authenticity of this last statement. It sounds to me as if Czerny was being wise after the event: there *was* a perceptible change, which Czerny would have felt, from the early sonatas (including the *Moonlight*) to the *Waldstein* and the *Appassionata*[2] sonatas which were being written three years later. But it does strike me as rather comical – Beethoven pronouncing in this stiff tin-soldier manner – reminiscent, perhaps, of the German proverb 'Tomorrow, I am going to start a new life! (. . . But don't wake me too early)'.

[1] An excerpt from *Symphony No. 1 in C major*, op. 21 is included on the FIRST BEETHOVEN RECORD.
[2] A movement from *Piano Sonata in F minor, op. 57*, the *Appassionata*, is included on the SECOND BEETHOVEN RECORD.

Beethoven told Amenda in 1801 he was composing all kinds of music *except operas and sacred music*. In the year immediately following the *Heiligenstadt Testament*, branching out even further to try new media, he turned in precisely this direction, to opera and sacred music.

His only oratorio, a dramatic work for soprano, tenor and bass soloists, chorus and orchestra, known in English as *Christ on the Mount of Olives*, was written unusually quickly (for Beethoven) in a matter of a fortnight or so. Its first performance was at Beethoven's benefit concert on 5 April 1803, when his second symphony and third piano concerto were also introduced for the first time. (Although he was able to negotiate favourable terms with his publishers and consequently was far from destitute, Beethoven's financial position was strengthened from time to time by a benefit concert.) Beethoven had been engaged to write an opera for the Theater an der Wien, and the oratorio *Christ on the Mount of Olives*, written in a hurry as a novelty for his concert, served to introduce him to the difficulties involved in dramatic vocal composition. It is seldom performed now.

After an abortive attempt to get to grips with an opera to a libretto called 'The Vestal Flame', he chose eventually a libretto which certainly did take hold of his imagination, and was to occupy him on and off for the next eleven years. It was called *Léonore ou l'amour conjugal* ('Leonore or wedded love'), a libretto which during the foregoing eight years was set by three other composers. Written in French by Jean Nicholas Bouilly (1763–1842), it was translated and prepared for Beethoven's use by Joseph Sonnleithner (1766–1835) who had recently assumed the post of Secretary to the Court Theatres at Vienna.

It is the libretto of a 'rescue' opera, an opera in which high drama is engendered through rescuing the hero out of an apparently impossible situation. Beethoven had wanted to write such an opera after seeing *Lodoiska* in particular, and *Les deux Journées*, by Cherubini (1760–1842) in 1802. The latter opera, literally, 'The Two Days' is known in English as 'The Water-Carrier'. These were the first major 'revolution' operas to reach Vienna. Beethoven had a high regard for Cherubini's music and the post-revolution opera's exciting topicality appealed strongly to him. It appealed to the Viennese as well, and there followed a flood of French operas which became even more popular in Vienna than they were in Paris. Bouilly's libretto of *Les deux Journées* was considered by Beethoven to be one of the very best he knew. It deals with the events of two troubled days in 1800. In the hair-raising action of the plot there are frequent displays of commendable moral qualities, such as kindness and loyalty.

Realism in the drama was expected as a matter of the first importance in these 'revolution' operas, and Bouilly based the plot of *Léonore ou l'amour conjugal*, as he had his *Les deux Journées*, on an actual incident which took place during the Reign of Terror. The action of the opera was set in Spain instead of France to prevent precise identification and is concerned with how Leonore rescues her husband Florestan, a nobleman who has been unjustly imprisoned, from a dingy gaol for political prisoners. Dressing up as a man and assuming the name of Fidelio, she gets taken on as an assistant gaoler. The themes running through the drama are hope, freedom and a consecrated self-sacrificing love in marriage.

Although it is thought by many of Beethoven's biographers that in creating his noble heroine he had Eleonore von Breuning in mind, I find of more interest the fascinating possibility that the *real* Leonore and Florestan may have survived the Reign of Terror to recognize themselves on the operatic stage.[1]

---

[1] *The Beethoven Companion*, ed. Arnold and Fortune, London, Faber, 1971. Chapter 9, by Winton Dean, 'Beethoven and Opera', p. 341.

Figure 9 Interior of the Theater an der Wien, anonymous engraving, 1825 (Historisches Museum of the City of Vienna).

It was perhaps no coincidence that the libretti of *Christ on the Mount of Olives* and *Leonore*, which bear such a strong resemblance to one another in expressing the anguish and yearning for release of men committed to death, should so forcefully have appealed at that time to Beethoven. The texts and the situations contained in them were highly relevant to the man who only the previous year had *not* committed himself to die, when suicide seemed a reasonable choice. And as one writer[1] has recently pointed out, the texts which seem to have caused Beethoven much trouble in setting them to music were those which touched him most profoundly: the phrase, for example, from Christ's aria, 'Take his cup of sorrow from me', and the recitative and aria sung by the hero of the opera, Florestan: 'God! what darkness here . . . Oh cruel fortune . . . Yet God's will is righteous. In the springtime of my life happiness has fled from me. But I have done my duty'.

Fidelio[2] was Beethoven's only opera, and apart from its particular relevance to him as *one* musical solution at a personal point of crisis it had of course undisguised topical significance. So much so that the première, scheduled for 15 October in 1805, was delayed by the Viennese censorship and demands were made for changes in the libretto[3] – setting the action back in the sixteenth century – but after recourse to the Empress the ban was lifted, the censorship being persuaded that the opera was not intended to be inflammatory. Its première on 20 November, and the repeat performances the following two evenings were a failure. It was structurally unsatisfactory and felt to be far too long. But political events on the larger scale played against its success as well. Napoleon's army invaded Vienna just over a week before the performances, with the result that Beethoven's usual supporters and patrons, his natural public the aristocracy, had fled, and the première was given before an audience mostly composed of French officers. If the 'freedom fighting' idealism of it appealed to them, the burden of watching a long drama in a foreign language would appear to have been too sore for them to bear again. The second and third performances were to empty houses.

Beethoven thought of his opera, and referred to it, as *Leonore*, but the première was advertised by the management of the Theater an der Wien as *Fidelio oder*

[1]Alan Tyson, *The Musical Times*, February 1969, pp. 139–41.
[2]The prisoners' chorus from Act 1 of *Fidelio* is included on the FIRST BEETHOVEN RECORD.
[3]Arnold and Fortune, 1971, p. 338.

Figure 10 Prisoners' Chorus, Covent Garden production of Fidelio, 1961 (*Houston-Rogers*).

Die eheliche Liebe ('Fidelio or conjugal love') against his wishes.[1] They did not want the opera to be confused in the minds of the public with an earlier setting of the same libretto, which had been seen at another Viennese theatre the previous autumn.

The first performance convinced even his friends and staunchest supporters that the opera was too long. His critics said it was ineffective and repetitious. Beethoven, though strenuously defending every note of his score, eventually capitulated and agreed to cut its length and rewrite sections of it. A second stage version was performed twice in 1806 before it was withdrawn, and after what he found to be an extremely taxing salvage operation, Beethoven's definitive version was staged, at last successfully, in 1814. It had become a convincing dramatic work, but only after the libretto had been adapted first by Stephan von Breuning (1774–1827) and then by George Friedrich Treitschke (1776–1842), the latter being a poet with the practical experience necessary to sort out the problems. In the process however, Beethoven's magnificent heroine has been to some extent dehumanized. It was pointed out in a recent publication how Bouilly's libretto,

> concentrates on the personal drama of Leonore and Florestan; the other prisoners are little more than a background. The moral is not emphasized, but allowed to emerge through the action. Treitschke and Beethoven raise it from the particular to the universal and ram it home so hard that the hollow reverberations of a thumped tub are all but discernible . . . The prisoners, no longer restricted to a single chorus, play a much larger part and obviously symbolize for Beethoven the whole of suffering mankind. The finale with its general amnesty becomes a pattern of the day of judgement.
>
> (Arnold and Fortune, 1971, p. 366.)

If you go to orchestral concerts, or are used to listening to music on the radio you may have puzzled over the number of overtures which belong to the opera: there are four, the overture *Fidelio* and three others called *Leonore* (Nos. 1, 2 and 3). They date from various attempts of Beethoven's to create the right sort of atmosphere for the opening of the opera. With such a profusion of material

---

[1]Notwithstanding Röckel's assertion to the contrary, in *Beethoven, Impressions by his Contemporaries*, p. 65.

Figure 11 Prisoners' Chorus, Norwegian State Opera production, 1970 (Norsk Telegrambyrå A/S).

seemingly begging to be used, it became conventional in the second half of the nineteenth century to preface the action on stage with the overture *Fidelio* and, although there are strong dramatic grounds against doing so, to insert the overture *Leonore, No. 3* in between the two scenes of Act II. This practice gave both orchestra and conductor a second chance to shine, unencumbered by stage action. It has largely died out by now, although you may still see a production of *Fidelio* in which the old convention is allowed.

EXERCISE

Turn to the set book *Beethoven, Impressions by his Contemporaries*, and read pages 60–8.

The situation appears romanticized, but it conveys convincingly to me the anguish which the decision to re-work *Leonore* must have cost Beethoven. Basing your answers on this account note short answers to:

1 *Reasons for failure*
   (a)   What did Beethoven put it down to?
   (b)   What did the others feel?
2 What was *the lever* the princess used which finally persuaded Beethoven to agree to revise it? Incidentally, does this seem reasonable to you?

Do this before going on

SPECIMEN ANSWERS

1 (a)   Beethoven blamed the man who had sung Florestan, and saw nothing else at all as contributing to the opera's failure.
   (b)   The opera needed cuts, and particularly the fusing of the first two acts into one.
2 The memory of his mother whom he respected so highly. Reasonable? – I think so; in this situation a strong personal appeal, emotionally put, might well have been what compelled Beethoven to grapple with *Leonore* a second time.

Christ on the Mount of Olives was completed in time to be performed at Beethoven's concert on 5 April 1803; *Fidelio* occupied him from the end of the year to the autumn of 1805. Between them he composed his *Third Symphony*, the *Eroica*. Schindler writes that the idea of the symphony was said to have been suggested by Bernadotte, then French Ambassador at Vienna, who was a great admirer of Beethoven's.[1] In this instance the title is not a nickname: the original edition of the orchestral parts, which appeared after the symphony had been composed almost three years, in October 1806, did actually bear the inscription[2] *Sinfonia Eroica . . . composta per festeggiare il sovvenire di un grand Uomo* ('Heroic Symphony, composed to celebrate the memory of a great man'). The great man in question: Napoleon Bonaparte.

A privileged pupil of Beethoven's, Ferdinand Ries, was eye-witness to his rage when, hearing that Napoleon had declared himself Emperor, Beethoven apparently tore off the title-page of his symphony and flung it on the floor shouting something on the lines of, 'Now he also will tread all human rights underfoot, will gratify only his own ambition, will raise himself above all others and become a tyrant!' Beethoven's autograph score, i.e. the score in his own handwriting, has been lost, and Ries might have been referring to a copy which does survive on which a violent attempt *has* been made to scratch out the words 'entitled Bonaparte' from the title-page. In a letter to the Leipzig music publishing firm Breitkopf & Härtel, 26 August 1804, that is, three months after Napoleon's imperial coronation had taken place, Beethoven wrote (*Selected letters of Beethoven*, p. 58) referring to his new symphony which he was offering to them, 'The title of the symphony is really *Bonaparte*: and in addition

Figure 12 Leonora and the gaoler descend to Florestan's cell, by Herman Kaulbach (Staatsbibliothek, Preussischer Kulturbesitz Bildarchiv, Berlin).

Figure 13 John Vickers as Florestan, Covent Garden production of Fidelio, *February 1961 (Houston-Rogers).*

---

[1]But although this claim about the inspiration of the symphony is the most well known at present, A. K. Holland in the *Symphony*, ed. Ralph Hill, London, Penguin Books, 1949, p. 98 gives alternative suggestions.

It might be borne in mind that, though one of Napoleon's marshals, Bernadotte never was a particularly ardent admirer of Napoleon and eventually (as heir to the Swedish throne) he led an army against Napoleon.

[2]*Ludwig van Beethoven*, ed. J. Schmidt-Görg and H. Schmidt, London, Pall Mall Press, 1970, p. 38.

to all the other usual instruments it has the accompaniment of three horns – I think that it will interest the musical public.' And later that year he was considering dedicating his *Mass in C* to Napoleon. The dedication of the *Eroica* might have been altered in view of this, on account of something more than simply annoyance for his hero. The alteration foreshadowed perhaps the tendency which we have seen in the final revision of *Fidelio*, to dehumanize an individual in the move from the particular to the universal: from the particular, living hero Napoleon, to the memory and inspiration of great men in general.

We see the practical aspect of his dealings with a music publisher in the letter mentioned earlier from Beethoven to Breitkopf & Härtel: a description of compositions for sale and the prices to be paid for them. And all Beethoven mentions with regard to this magnificent symphony, the *Eroica*, which is on a vaster scale than any symphonic composition before it, and in which he makes the most heroic gesture of those troubled years, is the novelty of including three horns in the orchestra.

There is an interesting note on the length of the *Eroica*, and on that extra third horn part, in the first violin part of the first edition:[1]

> This symphony being purposely written much longer than is usual, should be performed nearer the beginning rather than at the end of a concert and shortly after an overture, an aria and a concerto: so that if heard too late it will not lose for the listener already tired out by previous performances, its own proposed effect. The part of the third horn is arranged in such a manner that it can be played equally on the first horn or on the second.

> (Georg Kinsky, 1955, p. 129, quoted in H. C. Robbins Landon, 1970, p. 152.)

Perhaps I have said enough to encourage you to listen to the *Eroica* when you get an opportunity (it is not on the records provided). Be warned, however, against the kind of programme note which sees it as the biography of a hero. It would be a very peculiar one anyway, because the 'hero' is carried off dead as early as the second of the four movements. The *marcia funebre*, strengthening the French connection (before it was repudiated) is indebted to the influence of the slow marches played at funerals, which had become popular in France during the revolution.

Before continuing, look up the account I referred to by Ries. It is in *Beethoven, Impressions by his Contemporaries* pages 53 and 54, and is worth reading as the source of the best-known story about Beethoven and Napoleon. The account is plausible enough of Beethoven's reaction to the news, though I wonder whether his outburst isn't too idealistic to be spontaneous, while the more down-to-earth reaction attributed to him by another writer[2], 'Even with that bastard I made a mistake', might be closer to the mark.

Do this before going on

EXERCISE

It is time you checked to see how much of this section you have retained. If you cannot complete the answers very briefly, and get them right, in under half an hour you might profitably read the relevant pages again before proceeding.

---

[1]On the number of horn parts usually found in Beethoven's scores, see p. 92 of these units.
[2]Friedrich Kerst, *Die Erinnerungen an Beethoven*, Vol. 2, Stuttgart, 1913, p. 192, quoted in H. C. Robbins Landon, 1970, p. 202.

1 Whilst recognizing that the division of Beethoven's output into separate periods is a historical convenience more than a musical reality, what was the approximate extent of each of the three periods?

2 For what was Beethoven renowned in the early period?

3 How did he behave towards his public?

4 In what ways did Beethoven's professional status differ from that of most previous musicians?

5 Can you give three examples of his professionalism as a man living by his music?

6 What is the spirit which characterizes much of his music in the early period?

7 Most of Beethoven's compositions in the early period were written for the piano, or at least included a part for it. Suggest why.

8 In what ways did the scale and annual quantity of Beethoven's compositions change after 1800?

9 Earlier on we looked at three possibilities which Beethoven saw as alternative solutions to his predicament, when he realized he was faced with the prospect of a permanent disability. Can you remember what these were?

10 The *Heiligenstadt Testament* is a moving document written in the form of a will; why is it so called, when was it written, who was it addressed to? Why did Beethoven write it?

11 Beethoven's music took on a heroic quality around this time (1801–5). Which were the main works I described as exemplifying this?

12 Can you give three possible reasons why Beethoven's opera was not a success at first, despite the fact that the rescue opera, with themes drawn from actual experiences during the French Revolution, was then in vogue?

Do this before going on

Figure 14 Napoleon in his study 1812, by Jacques-Louis David (Kress Collection, National Gallery of Art, Washington).

SPECIMEN ANSWERS

1   See pages 13 and 15.

2   See page 15.

3   See pages 10 and 14.

4   See page 13.

5   See pages 13 and 14.

6   See pages 12 and 14.

7   Beethoven also played the violin and viola, you will remember, but it was as a virtuoso *pianist* he was renowned. He wrote his more demanding virtuoso piano music for his own use as he stood to gain both ways, as performer and composer, through concentrating his energies on what he would do best. He understood the medium, and because he used it so well he was personally much in demand at aristocratic soirées.

8   See page 24.

9   See page 23.

10 The answers to most of the points raised in the question are on pages 21 and 22. As to *why* Beethoven wrote the *Heiligenstadt Testament*, this is a more complex matter and your ideas are probably as good as mine! Beethoven seems to have felt so strongly that he was misunderstood, on account of the predicament he was in, that he had to give an explanation for his behaviour. He does this in a way which might induce his brothers to feel sympathetically for him, with the result that, hopefully, they would make it publicly known how he had suffered. Extending this, it could be said that he was writing for posterity. The *Heiligenstadt Testament* is an attempt to prove he had been unjustly regarded as a misanthrope. The document has also the function of a will, allowing Beethoven the opportunity to give his younger brothers advice about living virtuously and in harmony with one another. While naming them heirs to his effects, he optimistically requests that they agree between themselves which of them should have the set of very fine instruments he had been given by Prince Lichnowsky: a violin by Amati, a viola dated 1690, and both a violin and a cello by Guarneri.

11 See pages 25 and 29.

12 See pages 26–8.

The new heroic spirit, which I have drawn your attention to, may be seen emerging particularly in the oratorio *Christ on the Mount of Olives*, in *Fidelio* and the *Eroica* symphony. One must be wary, however, of reading too much of the life into the music. Although Beethoven was passing through an extremely distressing period of adjustment, while becoming resigned to permanent deafness, his music might seem to have been created in a context that was completely different from that of his suffering and the daily irritation of his latest illness. Having read about the struggle you might have expected evidence of it to be clearly discernible. In fact it is not so very obvious; but what *is* obvious is that by 1803, in the *Eroica*, and 1804, in the two famous piano sonatas, the *Waldstein* and the *Appassionata* for example, Beethoven's style is different from that of his early music.

It sounds far less like the music of Mozart and Haydn, and in spirit their music and his have only occasional resemblances. This difference in *spirit* is more than a normal generation gap (which after all one gets between Haydn and Mozart) and expresses what has happened not just to Beethoven, but to Europe, between 1795 and 1803. It gets into Mozart too – in the radical feeling of the operas (their plots especially) – but Mozart for all his intuitive sympathy with the radical spirit operates aesthetically within the framework of aristocratic culture, whereas Beethoven works his way through to an aesthetic equivalent of the new social developments.

You can probably bring to mind an instance when you have been put off someone by, perhaps, the way he talks although what he actually has to say is reasonable enough. You might well be put off by Beethoven's confident manner. Perhaps you don't like the style which he came to at the beginning of the nineteenth century, which I've interpreted as heroic. Perhaps the music strikes you as so much empty rhetoric. Irrespective, however, of how we might choose to describe Beethoven's music in 1803 and 1804, we must recognize that it is *different* from his music composed in the early 1790s. After an interim period of ten years we would not expect him to be repeating himself. But the change is not only that he is concerned with different kinds of things: he is also saying what he has to say in a new way.

It is not easy to define how the spirit of Beethoven's music differs from Haydn's, for instance. And unless you have listened to the music of both my definition won't mean much to you. Certainly, it would be better for you to put on a movement from one of the Beethoven records provided, and then to listen to some Haydn or Mozart on the radio. Try doing this, if you can. The immediacy of it can't be matched by any verbal description I could make.

Haydn was an enormously productive composer. His facility and deftness of touch contrast sharply with Beethoven's more laboured style of writing. Shortly you will be reading about Beethoven's methods of working, and will realize that although his music may seem to move on inevitably in absolutely the *right* way, he did not achieve this effect without a great deal of effort. He certainly didn't have Haydn's facility, and apart from in his easy drawing-room music this impression does not come over either. It is possible – though not justifiable – to consider Haydn's facility as a screen for a kind of happy vacuousness, but Beethoven's style, particularly from the middle period onward, could hardly be so regarded. Even when the music is of a light nature one may recognize in it a sense of authority the natural response to which is to take it seriously. There seems to be a seriousness of purpose in his music which does not make itself felt *in the same way* in the music of Haydn and Mozart.

It would be untrue to say that Mozart was not equally serious about the *Jupiter* symphony, for example, or the great *String Quintet in G minor* while he was composing them, as Beethoven was with any of his major compositions. Equally, it would be invidious to imply that just because he could write a symphony straight off in full score it was necessarily worth less attention than one of Beethoven's which he had spent months working on. The distinction I want to make cannot be completely divorced from each composer's facility of technique, but the question is, what impression does the music make upon you: does it provide a polite diversion for your wandering attention or something more; does it insinuate itself into your favour with agreeable effects or proceed, with little introduction or ceremony, in an assertive 'take it or leave it' manner?

If you are familiar with the dramatic style of the time of Haydn, Mozart and Beethoven, you might expect to be nudged every now and again as the composer repeats, '*Are you listening?*', and at every successive peak of expressive intensity seems to be inquiring, '*Are you with me?*' If this music is not exciting in its dramatic opposition of forces, different qualities of sound and orchestral 'colour', of keys and of themes, of the expected against the unexpected, it does not succeed on its own terms. Mozart and Beethoven succeed differently, Mozart being perhaps musically more polite than Beethoven.

Of course, I know dozens of exceptions will spring to a musician's mind to contradict my generalization. I myself could argue that most of the points I've made for Beethoven could be applied to Mozart as well. In many movements of Mozart we may imagine an impatient and fiery temperament but even in these (and certainly, taking his output as a whole) I feel that there is a seemliness which is absent in Beethoven's music. Beethoven's early compositions are full of self-confidence. It was his lack of regard for the conventional tenets of 'musical decorum', in the third of his op. 1 piano trios, which perturbed Haydn and led him to recommend that it should not be published. It was too forceful and disturbing for him. As it turned out, society was not unwilling to reconsider what was decorous and what was not. It was having at that time to reconsider so much more. Beethoven's third piano trio and far more controversial music became accepted and played with enthusiasm, notwithstanding some objection in the process of getting accepted, as in this newspaper account[1] of the first private performance of the *Eroica*.

> This lengthy composition, extremely difficult to perform, is in effect a very elaborate, audacious and wild fantasy. It is by no means lacking in striking and beautiful passages in which one recognizes the energetic, highly talented spirit of its creator; very often, however, it seems to lose its way in complete disorder . . . This reviewer is certainly among Herr van Beethoven's most sincere admirers, but he must say of this work that he finds too much that is harsh and bizarre in it, so that it is extremely difficult to view as a whole, and unity is almost entirely lost.
>
> (From the *Allgemeine Musikalische Zeitung*, Leipzig, February 1805, in Schmidt-Görg and Schmidt, 1970, p. 39.)

And after hearing it a second time the reviewer suggested:

> the Symphony would gain immeasurably (it lasts for a whole hour) if Beethoven would decide to shorten it, and bring more light, clarity and unity into the whole.

It is really quite a perspicacious review despite the fact that what the reviewer seems to be saying is that he has a very high regard for Beethoven's music but finds it incomprehensible and should like the *Eroica* to be more like a Haydn or Mozart symphony. Certainly the *Eroica* is long: the first movement alone lasts about as long as other complete, full-length symphonies before it, and it *is* technically difficult to perform.

Music had been getting more and more exclusively the preserve of the professional musician (and the good, trained amateur) throughout the second half of the eighteenth century: as the general standard of competence in instrumental playing was rising, new opportunities were being offered for composers to exploit technical expertise in more difficult pieces. And although Beethoven optimistically refused to believe it, gone were the days when a composer could hand out the parts of his new work and expect to hear a *performance* of it there and then, as had been possible earlier in the eighteenth century. Accounts of first performances of Beethoven's works make curious reading, and leave one asking *why?* to so many things. These first performances were usually terrible; players lost their places because they could not follow Beethoven's beat, or the parts had been so hastily scrawled they couldn't read them, the music was difficult and Beethoven became annoyed when the musicians were not able to play it properly first time, and there seems never to have been enough rehearsal before a performance.

But in addition to the personal difficulties each instrumentalist had to overcome, there were problems of ensemble which affected the whole orchestral body.

---

[1] From the *Allgemeine Musikalische Zeitung*, Leipzig, February 1805, in Schmidt-Görg and Schmidt, 1970, p. 39.

Critics said that his first symphony sounded more like a military-band piece than a symphony. Beethoven had handled his resources in a novel way, giving more prominence than had been customary to the woodwind instruments. The same criticism could, in fact, be applied to all of his orchestral music, and his contemporaries recognized that it was the use made of wind instruments which contributed characteristically to the novelty of the Beethoven sound. We'll be looking at this in more detail later (pp. 89–92).

During his first years in Vienna (1792–8) Beethoven had chosen to write for the media he understood best, and naturally his own instrument figured prominently in these early works. On the large scale, he had written two piano concertos. The concerto was a composition which, in a rather different form, had been current for well over a century. Noticeably, he had avoided writing in the *newer* large-scale genre, the symphony, until he had gained considerable experience in composition. He had been in the city six years before he took up the challenge and similarly, despite a generous commission to write string quartets, he had put off doing so until this time too. It was only towards the end of the early period that he seems to have felt ready to face Haydn and Mozart in the field in which they had proved themselves such masters.

> . . . with the one prominent (and inevitable) exception of the piano concerto, all the genres that Beethoven first controlled were those not specially favoured by the other two Viennese masters. Their piano trios and variations, and even their sonatas, are on the whole secondary works. They scarcely wrote at all for the string trio, the combination by which Beethoven first broke free of the piano. But with the string quartet, the symphony, the Mass, oratorio, and opera – here he moved into formidable competition with Haydn and Mozart in the forms they had cultivated with full responsibility and artistic intensity.

(Joseph Kerman, *The Beethoven Quartets*, London, Oxford University Press, 1967, p. 11.)

In 1798 taking the string quartet first and then almost two years later the symphony, Beethoven devoted his attention almost entirely to composing in these genres. The symphonies written subsequently are now played more frequently than the first. The op. 18 quartets are likewise overshadowed by the immensity of his achievement in the 'late' quartets[1] (though on account of the technical difficulty of the latter, this is not to say that the op. 18 quartets are played less than the 'late' ones). But it was by no means a battle lost – if battle it was – rather were new territories gained, from which the expanse of the quartets and symphonies he subsequently composed might be viewed more realistically.

The years from 1802 up to 1815 saw the composition of most of the music for which Beethoven is famous today.

Even if you wouldn't consider yourself to be musical, or if you don't listen to much music, some of these compositions, at least, would probably strike you as familiar if you heard them. They figure consistently often in concert programmes, and are available under a variety of record labels.

Symphonies nos. 2, 3 (*Eroica*), 4, 5, 6 (*Pastoral*), 7, 8 and the once popular, noisy money-raiser, the *Battle* symphony;

Piano Concertos nos. 3, 4 and 5 (*Emperor*);

Fantasia for piano, chorus and orchestra;

The Violin Concerto, and two Romances for violin and orchestra;

---

[1]The string quartets composed during the last three years of his life. These are referred to on pp. 100–2.

Triple concerto, for piano, violin, cello and orchestra;

The oratorio *Christ on the Mount of Olives* and the Mass in C;

The opera *Fidelio*, several overtures and a wide variety of miscellaneous vocal music;

Music for the theatre (including settings for Goethe's *Egmont*, and the ballet *Prometheus*);

Seven violin sonatas (including the *Kreutzer*) and three for cello;

Fourteen piano sonatas (including the *Waldstein*, *Appassionata* and *Les Adieux*) and 8 bagatelles for piano (including *Für Elise*);

Five string quartets (including the *Harp* and the three Razumovsky quartets);

Three piano trios (including the *Ghost* and the *Archduke*).

This is not an exhaustive list of his compositions but Beethoven did not write much more during the middle period. Considering this, it is an indication of his stature that the majority of these works are played today, most of them as often as any composition of the same genre by any other composer.

EXERCISE

A quick question to make sure we understand each other on the use of these technical terms. If you don't see any problem here skim the next paragraph or two.

Give a *very brief* definition of each of the kinds of composition listed above. For example, *Symphony*, a large-scale work, usually in four movements, for full orchestra.

Do this before going on

ANSWERS

You might have defined them on the following lines:

Piano concerto: a piece for full orchestra and solo piano, generally in three movements, lasting about the same length of time as a symphony – that is, half an hour or even more. The piano part is technically difficult, containing brilliant passages often of a bravura nature – exhibitionist, even. The word *concertante* has been applied to such writing. In the violin sonata dedicated to Kreutzer, Beethoven uses this word to describe a style approaching that of a concerto, adding a new dimension to the sonata by bringing to it something of the virtuoso display usual in the concerto. In a concerto the soloist sometimes plays with the orchestra sometimes alternates with it, seeming to be in opposition to it.

Fantasia: in this context a piece which is not in a set conventional form, but we might expect the composer to be giving rather free reign to his fantasy in a dramatic or ruminative kind of way.

For *Violin Concerto*, see the short definition above of piano concerto and substitute violin for piano. The solo violin, which plays most of the time and has the lion's share of memorable melodic material, is both supported by, and contrasted with, the orchestra. A *Romance* is a piece which usually has an obviously tender and intimate character.

Triple concerto: instead of one there are three soloists who share the leading parts: they may play in turn or all together, as well as with the full orchestra.

Figure 15 Beethoven miniature by H. C. Horneman, 1802 (Beethovenhaus, Bonn, Collection of Dr. H. C. Bodmer).

It was an unusual combination at the time (1805); from the beginning of the nineteenth century concertos normally had only *one* virtuoso soloist, although earlier it had been usual for as many as three or four players to take solo parts together.

Oratorio: a large-scale choral work. Generally, though not invariably, it was based on a religious text. It is a dramatic kind of composition, with sections contrasting the chorus with the vocal soloists. By the eighteenth century, oratorio was performed without scenery and stage action. This, and the nature of the libretto, differentiates *oratorio* from *opera*, which is always acted in costume, on stage with scenery.

Sonata: a composition for one instrument (e.g. piano) or two (e.g. violin and piano), usually in three or four movements. Beethoven's sonatas are sometimes more than half an hour in length. For Beethoven the term *sonata* would probably have meant a serious work for the keyboard (with or without other instruments), at least one movement of which was in sonata form. (I don't give an exhaustive definition of *sonata form* in these units, but see pp. 79–80.)

Bagatelle: as the French word suggests, it is a trifle, a short, light and often sweet little piece.

String quartet: a description of the medium as well as the kind of composition; a work which might last half an hour, in four movements usually, for two violins, a viola and a cello. From the end of the eighteenth century it had emerged as the most ambitious chamber medium; the equivalent in chamber music to the symphony as the vehicle of expression favoured for a composer's most seriously-considered music.

Piano trio: a piece for piano, violin and cello, in three or four movements, again usually around half an hour in duration.

As Beethoven boasted in his letters to Wegeler and Amenda, he was able to earn good money by his compositions. But he was annoyed that his work was not receiving more attention in Vienna. *Fidelio* was a failure in 1805 and was to suffer no better success in 1806. The public was reticent in its reactions to the *Eroica* as well, but although Beethoven's reputation continued to grow after that, and he certainly had the occasional success, he had become bitter with the Viennese.

Like a political leader forcing an issue to see just how much support he had, Beethoven contrived to obtain a *public vote of confidence*.

I don't believe he had seriously thought of leaving Vienna for good, but used the offer of a post he'd had, much as a professional man might these days mention how he had been pressed to accept an attractive post abroad, in order to get a substantial salary increase at home. Napoleon's brother, Jérôme Bonaparte, King of Westphalia, offered him the directorship of his court music on very attractive terms of employment. *Beethoven accepted the offer*, and on 7 January 1809 was writing to the Leipzig music publishing firm of Breitkopf & Härtel about going to take up his appointment as *Kapellmeister* to the Court at Kassel.

> At last owing to intrigues and cabals and meannesses of all kinds I am compelled to leave . . . I have accepted an offer from His Royal Majesty of Westphalia to settle there as Kapellmeister at a yearly salary of 600 gold ducats – I have just sent off by today's post my assurance that I will go, and am only awaiting my certificate of appointment; whereupon I shall make my preparations for the journey, which will take me through *Leipzig* – Therefore, so that the journey may be all the more glorious for me, I request you, provided that this is not too much to your disadvantage, not to make any of my compositions known to the public *until Easter*.

> . . . Abusive articles about my latest concert will perhaps be sent again from here to the Musikalische Zeitung. I certainly don't want everything that is written against me to be suppressed. But people should bear in mind that nobody in Vienna has more private enemies that I have. This is the more understandable since the state of music here is becoming worse and worse – We have Kapellmeisters who not only do not know how to conduct but also can hardly read a score – Conditions are worst of all, of course, at the Theater auf der Wieden – I had to give my concert there and on that occasion obstacles were placed in my way by all the circles connected with music – The promoters of the concert for the widows, out of hatred for me, Herr Salieri being my most active opponent, played me a horrible trick. They threatened to expel any musician belonging to their company who would play for my benefit – In spite of the fact that various mistakes were made, which I could not prevent, the public nevertheless applauded the whole performance with enthusiasm – Yet scribblers in Vienna will certainly not fail to send again to the Musikalische Zeitung some wretched stuff directed against me – The musicians, in particular, were enraged that, when from sheer carelessness a mistake had been made in the simplest and most straightforward passage in the world, I suddenly made them

stop playing and called out in a loud voice: '*Once more*.' – Such a thing had never happened to them before. The public, however, expressed its pleasure at this – But every day things are getting worse . . .

Please do not make public anything definite about my appointment in Westphalia until I let you know I have received my certificate – Accept my good wishes and write to me soon – We shall discuss the question of new works at Leipzig – Of course, a few hints about my leaving Vienna might be inserted in the Musikalische Zeitung – and with the addition of a few digs, seeing that people here would never do anything worth mentioning for me – . . .

(*Selected letters of Beethoven*, pp. 81–3.)

That he had accepted this offer and appeared to be on the point of packing up and going, so dismayed his Viennese supporters that they requested him to make a clear statement of what he would like, to make it acceptable for him to remain amongst them. This led to a contract being signed on 1 March 1809, under which agreement Beethoven undertook to remain in Vienna as his permanent home in return for a guaranteed annual income of 4,000 florins.

The gold ducat was then worth about 4½ florins, so the Viennese salary of 4,000 florins a year was a sizeable increase on the Kassel bid, in terms of florins, of about 2,700 florins salary plus 675 florins travelling expenses, a total of 3,375 florins.

Three aristocrats undertook to pay Beethoven's annuity. These guarantors were, needless to say, devoted admirers of his music and, as was often the case in aristocratic circles, themselves practising amateur musicians. Ferdinand Bonaventura, Prince Kinsky (1781–1812) was to make a yearly contribution of 1,800 florins, the Archduke Rudolph (1788–1831) 1,500 and Prince Franz Joseph von Lobkowitz (1772–1816) 700.

In parenthesis, we might refer to a letter by the German composer Johann Friedrich Reichardt (1752–1814), written at Vienna, 10 December 1808, describing an amateur concert which he had just attended. This would have corresponded exactly to the time when Beethoven was considering the call to Kassel. Reichardt recounts what he felt like on hearing Beethoven's overture *Coriolan* (op. 62).

My brain and my heart almost burst from the hammer blows and shrillness within the narrow rooms, especially as everyone tried with all his might to increase the noise in view of the fact that the composer was present. It gave me great pleasure to see dear Beethoven being much fêted, particularly because he has the unfortunate, hypochondriac whim that everyone here persecutes and despises him. His highly obstinate character may well scare off many of the kind-hearted and gay Viennese. And even among those who recognize his great talent and achievement, there are few who have enough humanity and subtlety to offer the sensitive, easily aroused and suspicious artist the means to grasp the pleasant side of life, so that he might happily accept it and find in it satisfaction as an artist. It really upsets me very deeply when I see this basically good and remarkable man looking gloomy and suffering, although I am convinced, on the other hand, that his best and most original works can only be produced when he is in a stubborn and deeply morose state of mind. Those people who are able to enjoy his works should never lose sight of this and not let themselves be put off by his outward peculiarities and rough edges. Only then can they be his true and sincere admirers.

(Johann Friedrich Reichardt, *Vertraute Briefe*, ed. G. Gugnitz, Munich, 1915, Vol. 1, p. 174, quoted in H. C. Robbins Landon, 1970, pp. 215–6.)

But, though Beethoven's income was *guaranteed*, little was certain during the Napoleonic Wars, and when the Austrian Empire became bankrupt and introduced an emergency measure devaluing paper currency in February 1811, Beethoven's 4,000 florin income was reduced to the value of approximately 1,600. Archduke Rudolph was able to increase his contribution but Prince Lobkowitz, for four years, could make no contribution at all, and the situation became even more difficult the following year in 1812 when the third and most heavily committed guarantor, Prince Kinsky, died after falling from his horse. His contribution to the annuity was however only temporarily stopped, his family resumed payment after a disagreeable law suit had been fought on Beethoven's behalf. And eventually the value which the annuity was intended to have was restored when payment was made in a new kind of currency.[1]

Although they were troubled times for everybody, staying on in Vienna did bring at last the satisfaction for Beethoven of being lionized as never before. His music enjoyed tremendous success during the Congress of Vienna in 1814. *Fidelio* was well received, and in November he had a triumphant benefit concert, called a 'Grand Musical Academy' in the Imperial Redoutensaal. The concert was scheduled to take place on Sunday 27 November, a time which it was assumed would be convenient for the great number of aristocratic delegates then in Vienna, but an amusing report to the Viennese Secret Police explains why it was postponed until the following Tuesday: 'The English are so religious that they do not listen to music on Sundays. Therefore the musical Academy of Herr van Beethoven was postponed from Sunday to a weekday . . .' (H. C. Robbins Landon, 1970, p. 282).

As usual on occasions like this, Beethoven let the public hear a novelty as well as his most recent large-scale compositions. One novelty was a choral work. It was entirely topical in fact, being a setting of a poor text, called (in translation) *The Glorious Moment*, about how many sovereigns there were then in Vienna. The concert opened with his *Seventh Symphony*. But the real success item, which had been received with great acclaim since it had first been heard the previous year, was *Wellington's Victory or The Battle of Vittoria* (op. 91). *The Battle Symphony*, as it became known, was originally written for the *panharmonicon*, a large and ingenious mechanical organ constructed by J. N. Maelzel (1772–1838), inventor of the metronome. In addition to instigating the composition of the piece, Maelzel seems to have had a hand in its design as well, and the intention was that he and Beethoven should go over to England to put it on in various cities. It was to be a money-raiser on a predictably popular topical theme. The plan fell through, however, and after Beethoven had scored it for orchestra, and had it performed with great success at a concert for the benefit of wounded soldiers, in Vienna, he and Maelzel came into dispute over what rights each of them had on the composition. At all events, Maelzel more than recouped the money owing to him by Beethoven and what was due to him for various ear trumpets he'd made for him, by taking an orchestral version (which Beethoven maintained he'd stolen) to Munich and elsewhere.

Although he could not go to England at that time (in fact he never managed it) Beethoven hoped that he should have some financial gain from his *Battle Symphony*.

He dedicated it to the Prince Regent and sent him a copy in April 1814 without first, however, having inquired whether he would accept the dedication. To Beethoven's annoyance, while he heard that the battle music was being enthusiastically received in London, he received no acknowledgment of the dedication from the prince. Nor was the money which in such circumstances was conventionally paid to the composer in recognition of the honour of the dedication forthcoming. In 1823 Beethoven was still trying to make *something* out of it, writing (*Selected letters of Beethoven*, p. 202) to the prince who by then had become King George IV: 'For many years the undersigned cherished the agreeable hope that Your Majesty would most graciously have him informed of

[1]*Selected Letters of Beethoven*, see 'Notes on money values', pp. xv–xvi.

Figure 16 'Wellington's Victory or the Battle of Vittoria', op. 91, title-page (Beethovenhaus, Bonn).

the safe arrival of his work. But as yet he has not been able to boast of his happiness . . .'

The *Battle Symphony*, put together to exhibit spectacular effects on a glorified musical box, and surely one of Beethoven's most banal compositions, became the piece which brought him the greatest renown during his own lifetime. There is a nice shift of allegiance here too – though not one, I think, to be pondered over too deeply – from Beethoven's first dedicating a symphony to Napoleon, then deciding not to, and now celebrating a victory of Wellington's over the French.

EXERCISE

Would you turn now to J. W. N. Sullivan's *Beethoven* (originally published by Jonathan Cape in 1927, now by Allen & Unwin, London, 1964) and *read and consider* Chapter VI, entitled 'Love and Money', pages 106–26. Make a note of your answers.

1 In Beethoven's middle period, what general characteristic or spirit might you find in his music?
2 What is the date Sullivan gives as the beginning of Beethoven's unproductive period?
3 From then on what happened by way of change in the spirit of his music?
4 Sullivan does not actually attribute Beethoven's unproductiveness during this period to particular causes, but shows that it coincides with some. Which does he mention?
5 Although it seems that Beethoven felt strongly that he wanted to get married, it is suggested that he really feared the consequences of doing so. Why?
6 What outcome did his not getting married have in his music?
7 How long did the financial arrangement made to persuade Beethoven to remain in Vienna last?
8 Throughout his discussion Sullivan emphasizes that in whatever he did

Beethoven was true to himself. How does he justify Beethoven's dealings with his music publishers?

9 On his dealings with music publishers, is it suggested
   (a) that Beethoven was blameless?
   (b) that his code of morals was misunderstood?

Do this before going on

ANSWERS

I will not paraphrase or condense Sullivan. You will find the relevant passages on the pages I refer to.

1 Page 106.
2 Page 106.
3 Pages 106, 107.
4 Pages 107, 114, 120, 121.
5 Pages 115, 116.
6 Pages 116, 117.
7 Pages 117, 118 and correspondence text page 39.
8 Pages 119, 124–6.
9 (a) No   (b) Pages 124–6.

For a biographical guide to the remaining years of Beethoven's life let's turn to Alan Tyson's succinct account, from his introduction to *Selected Letters of Beethoven*:

On 15 November 1815 Beethoven's brother Caspar Carl died of consumption; under his will he appointed Beethoven guardian of his son, Karl, who was nine years old. It is clear that he feared disharmony between the boy's mother and Beethoven, for a codicil, which he signed the day before his death, added his wife as co-guardian. 'God permit them to be harmonious for the sake of my child's welfare. This is the last wish of the dying husband and brother.' Harmonious! An immense amount of Beethoven's time, energy, and emotion were spent in the next ten years in battles conducted at a personal level and through the courts to get himself recognized as sole guardian, and to remove the boy from all contact with his mother, whom he persistently charged with immorality and referred to as the 'Queen of the Night'. For it came about that all Beethoven's frustrated desire for family ties and parenthood, his possessiveness and his demand to receive and to be able to give affection, were concentrated on this rather decent and patient adolescent. The letters to Karl written in 1825 make painful reading; week by week the tension increased till in July 1826 Karl, not yet twenty, tried to escape from Beethoven's constant scenes of reproach and the torment of divided loyalties by attempting to shoot himself. He was unsuccessful, but he made his point; Beethoven renounced the guardianship and Karl entered the army.

How much music was lost to Beethoven and to us as a result of these struggles over his nephew is hard to estimate. Certainly the pace of creation was slower, and long periods elapsed in which he composed hardly anything. Yet these were also the years of the last five piano sonatas, the Choral Symphony and the Mass in D (the 'Missa Solemnis'). This last work, originally intended for the enthronement of the Archduke Rudolph as an archbishop in 1819, was not completed till 1823. The devious negotiations over its publication (Beethoven seems to have offered it at various times to eight different publishers) had little to do with Beethoven's real financial circumstances, but were perhaps derived from his irrational fears of poverty, and his increasing suspiciousness: for the disingenuousness of the letters is very different from the openness that marked his earlier dealings with Hoffmeister or with Breitkopf & Härtel.

For although there was at last a realization among the Viennese – touchingly expressed in a petition of 1824 urging him to give a concert of his latest works – that the greatest living composer was in their midst, Beethoven, who was now cut off by almost complete deafness and could carry on a discussion with visitors only through 'conversation books', was gradually withdrawing from human contacts. His character was deteriorating; his suspiciousness extended to all around him: servants (whom he could never keep for long), his nephew and sister-in-law, his devoted factotum Schindler. Now, with the additional burden of intermittent illness, he worked away at his last string quartets, which he completed one after another. By December 1826 it was clear that Beethoven was really ill. News of his condition spread far beyond Vienna; in February 1827 the Philharmonic Society of London sent a hundred pounds to relieve his distress. This reached Vienna in the middle of March, and it is pleasant to read his letter of thanks to Moscheles in London. Nine days after writing it, on 26 March 1827, he was dead; his nephew was his sole heir.

(*Selected letters of Beethoven*, Introduction.)

Beethoven's funeral on 29 March 1827 was felt to be one of those very great and solemn occasions which few of us ever live to see. It has been estimated however that on that occasion well over ten thousand people attended and the leading musicians in Vienna accompanied the bier. Schubert was one of them, and is said to have caught a cold there. He got rid of it, but he was dead himself in a year.

It was such an occasion when perhaps the dramatic gesture was not out of place and the crowd were made to feel this, when they heard the poet Franz Grillparzer's funeral oration (*Beethoven, Impressions by his Contemporaries*, pp. 229–31). It was read by an actor at the cemetery gates, and it ends, with sonorous reverberations of King Harry's haranguing of the troops upon Saint Crispin's day.

> remember this hour, and think, we were there, when they buried him; and when he died, we wept.

Beethoven's attitude towards convention, in social as much as musical matters, marked him particularly as a child of his time in the Age of Revolutions. He did not hold with the conventions of the old regime unless there was a good reason for doing so, certainly not for convention's sake. He was not a conventional person, as you have learned. And although he must have realized that his behaviour in society was most unusual he did not turn this to commercial advantage. He was completely true to himself: he knew that he was endowed with exceptional capabilities and wasn't embarrassed about it. Nor did he have any false modesty.

You may have heard the anecdote (see Schindler, 1966, p. 200) about how, in 1823, he received a New Year's card from his brother, who had signed himself 'Johann van Beethoven, landowner'. He immediately returned it, having written on the back 'Ludwig van Beethoven, brainowner'.

It is clear by all accounts that he was not an aristocratic lackey. But he wouldn't be taken for a peasant either. His direct appeal, then, was to the educated upper classes who were culturally equipped to appreciate his music. He had strong ideals about the brotherhood of man, but his own behaviour indicated that he saw himself as above the mob, in a position of unique privilege – of being a *creator*. He wasn't a democrat, really. In an elitist sort of way, he was a snob.

From around 1803 when deafness made his career as a virtuoso pianist impossible, he had been forced into becoming what was at that time a new kind of artist, a composer. From the number of his compositions, as compared with his old contemporaries, the obsessional care about every detail which we can see in the sketches, as well as the impression made by the music itself, it may be learned that Beethoven had very seriously committed himself to a life of composition. There is a new seriousness of purpose which the following generation of musicians, born around 1810 – Mendelssohn, Schumann, Wagner, Liszt and company – were to emulate. And although Beethoven didn't usually starve in a draughty garret, the idea of this great misunderstood musician dedicating his life to Art so completely, caught the romantic imagination and Beethoven was deified although much of his music was yet to be appreciated for what it was. Even Schindler who had been so close to him in the last years, failed to see the lasting greatness of his different compositions – going into extasies over the surface excitement of the *Battle Symphony* and *The Glorious Moment*, and even nostalgically when Beethoven was dead, writing (Schindler, 1966, p. 142) 'the reader may, of himself, draw this conclusion: that, if the first period of Beethoven's life may be justly called his golden age, that which immediately followed it was not a silver age, but an age of brass.'

Bringing this section to a close, here is an extract from the introduction to a distinguished collection of essays which was published to mark the bicentenary of the birth of Beethoven.

> The freeing of the individual from convention is always infinitely baffling and ambiguous, but the miracle of Beethoven's music is that in its liberty and individuality it is also finitely organic and compelling. In its caprice there lives the passionate logic of dissection and synthesis, in its dissolubility there is no looseness, for despite all its arbitrariness and its many crises, this music reaches final harmony.
>
> Today some young and impatient musicians find Beethoven objectionable; they are alienated by his security, by his imperious determination, they deride his majestic egotism, they resent his timelessness which still gives us lessons, but above all, they are dismayed by the eternal presence of the hero who cannot be undone. As each new generation comes along, it sees its own place in the sun as requiring the downfall of its predecessors and of their idols and heroes, so that rebirth can follow. The world needs rebels in order to be able to move and preserve its rhythm. Beethoven does represent the highest heroism precisely because the revolutionary character of his music is kept powerfully within bounds, the mind of the classically schooled craftsman is always in command, ordering and organizing. Bartók and Stravinsky were still full of admiration for Beethoven, but many of today's musicians are completely estranged from him; they misjudge Beethoven's heroism, its humanity, its intensity of expression and communication. It is this passion that gives Beethoven's music its heroic clangor, its rhetorical force.
>
> In the end, the grandeur and the heroism are Beethoven himself, the creative man who cannot be fulfilled, and it is this lack of complete creative fulfillment that paradoxically shows the richness of his soul. For he realized that he would never find the old Haydn's absolute peace, only relative calms in the struggle. This is what eternally drove him, from masterpiece to masterpiece, toward the unattainable fulfillment, and this is what creates in his music the great tensions that enthrall people all over the world.
>
> (*The Music Quarterly*, Vol. LVI, No. 4, October, New York, G. Schirmer, Inc., 1970, p. 514. Introduction by the editor, Paul Henry Lang.)

There are interesting accounts of Beethoven in later life in *Beethoven, Impressions by his Contemporaries*. You have probably browsed through some already. The ones by Tomaschek (p. 100), Potter (107), Rochlitz (120), Schlösser (132), Smart (191), Spiker (209) and Schindler's letters to Moscheles (212, 219) are the most reliable.

If you are well in hand with your work this week, you can profitably spend an hour or so reading these passages.

SECTION 2 ON BEETHOVEN'S PROCESS OF COMPOSITION

Figure 17 Crayon drawing of Beethoven, c. 1824 by Stefan Decker (Museum der Stadt Wien).

When Beethoven first made his mark it was as a virtuoso pianist. His technical assurance at the keyboard when he was a young man gained him the admiration of all who heard him perform, and he was held to be the finest pianist of his day. But it was not this outstanding technique but his gift for improvising that is said to have impressed Mozart so much when they met in Vienna in 1787. Later, when he had made Vienna his permanent home, and had been accepted as a distinguished, if rough and rather abrasive, young virtuoso in the round of aristocratic drawing rooms, he was eagerly pressed to improvise at the piano for his hosts. Even after becoming deaf, and it was known that this disability prevented him from playing cleanly, musicians thought themselves extremely fortunate if they could persuade Beethoven to improvise for them, or failing that, were able to trick him into doing so. There is an account, for example, in *Beethoven, Impressions by his Contemporaries*, page 115, of how an English visitor and his friends tricked Beethoven into letting them hear him improvise.

The qualities he characterized so strongly in his playing were an energetic daring and a completely personal kind of expressiveness. One musician who heard him in 1791, comparing his playing with that of another foremost virtuoso, the Abbé Vogler (1749–1814), said that Beethoven, 'in addition to the execution, has greater clearness and weight of idea, and more expression – in short, he is more for the heart – equally great, therefore, as an *adagio* or *allegro* player.' Another described how 'the creative genius gradually unveiled his profound psychological pictures . . . leaving the field of mere tonal charm, bodily stormed the most distant keys in order to give expression to violent passions.' (*Beethoven, Impressions by his Contemporaries*, pp. 13, 31.) It is difficult across the years to judge what these improvisations were really like although some impression may be gained from a little music of this kind which survives in written form. One thing is, however, quite certain, for accounts of his performance substantiate what the great pianist Carl Czerny (1791–1857) wrote, that

> no matter in what company he might be, he knew how to make such an impression on every listener that frequently there was not a single dry eye, while many broke out into loud sobs, for there was a certain magic in his expression, aside from the beauty and originality of his ideas and his genial way of presenting them.

> (*Beethoven, Impressions by his Contemporaries*, p. 31.)

Beethoven was a born showman, knowing instinctively what would suit his audience best, while yet (again according to Czerny) despising them for responding to his playing with sentimentality. A few pieces survive that may give us the feel of Beethoven's improvisatory style. If you have an opportunity, listen to the soloist in his *Fantasia for Piano, Chorus and Orchestra: op. 80*, or to the soloist again in the cadenzas Beethoven composed for his own use when he was performing Mozart's *D minor Piano Concerto, K.466*. Another such piece for piano solo is Beethoven's *Fantasia in G minor, op. 77*, a strange, forceful piece which impresses with its wayward changes of tonality. But if Beethoven's improvisations were like this (Czerny said that the op. 77 *Fantasia* gave a fair impression of one) how shall we view what Beethoven told the Bohemian composer Johann Wenzel Tomaschek when they met in 1814? Please turn to *Beethoven, Impressions by his Contemporaries* page 105 and read it, taking particular notice of the passage from 'It always has been acknowledged that the greatest pianists were also the greatest composers' to the end of Beethoven's statement.

Do this before going on

My reaction is to question the degree of integration achieved by Beethoven's 'real virtuosos'. Judging by the persistence with which Beethoven himself had to work at his musical ideas, and the difficulties he sometimes experienced which are obvious from his sketches at such times, I would not have expected him to have achieved in a spontaneous composition at the piano the same degree of interconnectedness and subtlety as he might, had he the opportunity to think the material over and alter his composition through a number of drafts.

Now from Beethoven's improvisations to his written-out compositions.

Beethoven composed by *manipulating* his musical ideas: either physically at the piano when he was improvising or, when working on a 'permanent' composition, visually on paper by means of a system of sketches in successive drafts.

Consider this letter which Beethoven wrote to his adopted son, Karl, on 11 August 1825.

I am in a mortal fright about the quartet. For Holz has taken away the third, fourth, fifth and sixth movements. But the first bars of the third movement are still here, that is to say, thirteen bars of it – I have heard nothing from Holz – I wrote to him yesterday. He usually writes. What a terrible misfortune if he has lost the manuscript. Between ourselves, he is a hard drinker. Make my mind easy as quickly as possible . . . [then he goes on to say *how* Karl might do this, by going to see someone, and ends the letter saying] . . . For God's sake do make my mind easy about the quartet, for that would be a terrible loss. The ideas for it are only jotted down on small scraps of paper; and I shall never be able to compose the whole quartet again in the same way.

Your faithful father.

(*Selected letters of Beethoven*, pp. 229–30.)

Beethoven was upset at the prospect of having lost a composition which had cost him considerable time and energy. The one in question was the second 'Galitzin' quartet: *String Quartet in A minor, op. 132*, and he certainly did not want anyone else illicitly to make money out of his efforts. You may remember that he liked to believe he lived entirely by the sale of his music. So proud was he of his status as an 'independent' artist that, so long as he continued to receive it, he preferred to put out of mind the annuity he had been getting since 1809 through the generosity of his aristocratic friends, Kinsky, Lobkowitz and the Archduke Rudolph. But apart from the financial aspect, the loss of the string quartet was an irremediable musical one as well for Beethoven because, as he writes, 'The ideas for it are only jotted down on small scraps of paper; and I shall never be able to compose the whole quartet again in the same way.' He does not suggest that he could not compose the quartet again, but that if ever he were to attempt it *the quartet would not be the same as the first version of it*. He was satisfied with the way the *String Quartet in A minor* had 'worked out' and in the unlikely event of his having to recompose it from the material which still remained, the end result might not have been as good.

What were these 'ideas jotted down on small scraps of paper'? How much of the quartet could have been salvaged from them, and were they only *ideas* as Beethoven says, or rather fuller, detailed drafts of the composition as it was to emerge?

Incidentally, although I have not found that learning about his working habits has increased the pleasure I get from listening to Beethoven's music or playing it, discovering how he composed *is* a fascinating study.

Remember that Beethoven, unlike musicians before him who had worked as 'all round' musicians (playing, composing and giving music lessons), was forced on account of his deafness to become a specialist *composer* and for the last twenty years at least, when social contacts had diminished, the practice of composition occupied him fully.

I am immensely impressed by how hard Beethoven worked. Perhaps, when you have followed him through the various stages in the act of composition, you may be too.

EXERCISE

To get some of the flavour of the age Beethoven lived in and to increase your familiarity with Beethoven as he is reported to us, look up the following passages in *Beethoven, Impressions by his Contemporaries*. Each refers to one or more aspects of how he went about the actual process of composing. After you have read them, pause to ask what kind of impression *you* have had, then note the details which seem to emerge as significant. The relevant pages are: 37, 42, 49, 53, 85, 100, 127, 152, 159, 167–9, 207, 211.

DISCUSSION

You have probably been struck as I was by the difference in style between these passages. Moreover, you can feel that whereas one author writes with authority and seems to be sticking to facts, another gives the impression that he is (with equal confidence) perpetuating exaggerations. After accepting that some accounts were not based on personal experience but on heresay, you might have noted which idiosyncrasies of Beethoven's seemed to you to be genuine.

The impression I have received on reading these colourful accounts may be considered under five points.

1 Beethoven did a certain amount of composition before actual recourse to paper,

    (a) thinking all the time of appropriate and workable ideas, 53, 126, 169, 211

    (b) arranging them in relation to one another, 37, 44

    (c) considering the overall shape of the movement, 152.

2 He jotted these ideas down

    (a) in lead pencil in his pocket book, 37, 42, 85, 211

    (b) which he *always* carried, 42, 49, 211

    (c) whenever they occurred to him, even in the middle of the night, 207.

3 In addition to these pocket-book jottings he worked in large books, writing in ink, 100, 211.

4 What he wrote in his sketch-books was written in such bad handwriting, and with such apparent lack of order about it, that the books *must* have been intended for his private use alone, 42, 100, 159.

And in conclusion:

5 For Beethoven the business of composing was carried on to a *systematic* routine. And it was a matter of serious, concentrated *hard* work.

Beethoven was probably the first composer to use sketches systematically, as indispensable to the creative process of composition. When he died Beethoven's belongings were sold by auction, amongst them his collection of conversation books and sketch-books, and these books have been accepted as characteristic appendages of the great man. One knew about the chronic deafness by which he was disabled. From the age of thirty it had been more than a social inconvenience; it had been getting steadily worse and eventually he could not hear anything. Consequently, the fact that people could only communicate with Beethoven through writing what they had to say in his notebook was an obvious reason for the existence of the many volumes in his possession recording one side only of a conversation. But, having accepted that Beethoven's conversation books were indispensable to him, musicians made the same assumption about his sketch-books – without really inquiring why this should be so. And although it was known that Beethoven had been in the practice of sketching out his compositions in various ways, and some scholars, of whom the most notable was Gustav Nottebohm, had drawn attention to this in the nineteenth century, it is only recently that it has become fairly generally understood, amongst music historians of this period, what function the sketch-books had.

The Sketches

His contemporaries were amused by Beethoven's idiosyncratic way of composing. There were frequent references, in the passages you have just read, to the urgency with which he wrote down on paper musical ideas as and when they occurred to him. When he was out of the house on his daily walks, ideas were jotted down in his pocket book, in pencil of course. These sketches are very rough indeed. They were obviously scribbled very hastily, and if we look at them we might not manage to recognize the ideas at all. From our point of view pitch is very haphazardly represented; clefs and key signatures are omitted, being taken for granted. The feature which offers the best clue to the identity of the idea is its rhythmic shape. These sketches are often very short fragments, embryonic motives for future development. If Beethoven needed to be reminded of the ideas he'd had while out walking, he would refer to his pocket book before noting them in a larger-sized manuscript book he had on his desk. His pocket-book scribblings were expendable once the ideas had been written in his desk book, and he probably threw them some of them away. Quite a lot survive, however, especially for the late quartets. The earliest pocket-book sketches still extant date from when Beethoven was about forty-five. The successive desk books, on the other hand, were the essential and continuing record of thought and he valued them so much that he preserve them carefully, even though one would think that he had ample temptation to be rid of them every time he moved his lodgings, which happened fairly frequently in Vienna besides his annual move out to the country every summer.

The sketches served perhaps partly to remind him what he had thought of, or perhaps they show how he was thinking on paper – a record of his soliloquizing on the material at hand. Ideas are noted down and altered in various ways; he searches to discover the structure which the movement must have as a result of the way his material has turned out; very occasionally he adds a comment in words. While working on the 'Pastoral' Symphony, for example, which he called 'reminiscences of country life', perhaps he was giving himself a warning not to overdo the signposting when he wrote '*Man überlässt es dem Zuhörer sich selbst die Situationen auszufinden*' ('Leave it to the listener to find the situations out for himself'). But such comments are few, and by far the greater part of these books is occupied by sketches in which melodic material is progressively refined and developed.

These sketches would have been written out very quickly, as in the pocket-book sketches: the handwriting is very untidy. Beethoven could write *fairly* neatly when he had to (although it takes some time for us to become accustomed to reading it), but this was a case when he didn't have to be tidy. His sketches were for his personal use alone and, obviously, he could understand his own musical shorthand. He did not waste time writing in music notation information which he did not need reminding of, like clefs, key signatures and time signatures, and only seldom did he indicate what he had in mind in the way of instrumentation, phrasing, or dynamics. What he was aiming at was a satisfactory working out of the material he had chosen. He concentrated for pages at a time on a single idea if necessary, writing it out time after time making slight alterations in pitch and rhythm until he must have liked what he'd arrived at.

With the more difficult details solved he had to adjust *the rate of action* of the music so that the shorter passages, which he had already worked out satisfactorily, should be truly integrated. 'I make many changes, reject and re-attempt until I am satisfied', Beethoven is reported to have said to Louis Schlösser, a young composer who had sought his guidance in 1823:

Then the working-out in breadth, length, height and depth begins in my head, and since I am conscious of what I want, the basic idea never leaves me. It rises, grows upward, and I hear and see the picture as a whole take shape and stand forth before me as though cast in a single piece, so that all that is left is the work of writing it down.

(*Beethoven, Impressions by his Contemporaries*, pp. 146–7.)

But writing it down in a form which others could understand was not the simple chore Beethoven implies it was, which followed after the real business of composition, the thinking-out of what went where. The sketches record some of the 'thinking-it-out' stages, but it is important to remember that a sketch for Beethoven was no more than the word suggests: it was just enough to remind him of the essential, which usually meant the most important melodic outline. Having refined his main thematic material at least sufficiently to allow him to get started. Beethoven experimented to find the most satisfactory *proportions* for the movement. As he told Schlösser, he might from fairly early on be conscious of what he wanted, but it required his becoming better acquainted with the possibilities offered by his material if he was to achieve his objective. So he manipulated it, presumably playing it over in his mind as he very quickly sketched out the main elements of the music *in a single line*, weighing up the balance of phrases, the pull of this key against the other, the relationship between passages of high tension and of relaxation, and so on. It is interesting to recall, in this connection, how Ferdinand Ries (1784–1838), who used to be his pupil, describes the painstaking care Beethoven took over teaching him how to integrate details of the composition he was *playing* into a satisfying whole. He insisted on making Ries repeat 'almost the entire final Adagio variation [of the *6 variations*, op. 34, for piano] seventeen times; and even then he was not satisfied with the expression in the small cadenza, though I thought I played it as well as he did.' (*Beethoven, Impressions by his Contemporaries*, p. 52.)

For Ries to repeat the cadenza out of context was obviously not good enough. He might practise it like that in order to get technical fluency but the musical, interpretive problem of integrating the cadenza with the fragmented and delicate writing which leads up to it, making the cadenza sound essential and inevitable, could only be solved through playing a longer passage – which meant the previous six bars at least and ideally the foregoing twelve.

When Beethoven had reached what has variously been called the stage of making his 'continuity draft' or 'unilinear sketch' (this is the sketch in which all the important elements are compressed into a single line), he was ready to bring his composition out into the open, as it were, by writing out a fully harmonized and fully scored version in conventional music notation. He had by no means finished composing at that stage as we shall see, but he had found the proportions of the movement and had probably a clear idea of the essential detail as well.

The sketches make three aspects of Beethoven's approach clear:
1 He made sure his melodic material consisted of short fragments which could be developed independently, as well as collectively in the form of a recognizable main tune.
2 In the early stages he was more concerned with getting the structure right than with thinking about how he should contrast the sonorities of the instruments involved. First the form; the colour came later.
3 And similarly, as basic to the structure of the movement, it was more important for him to work out where modulations[1] should take place than to harmonize short passages in detail.

[1]If you don't know what such technical terms as this one mean, consult a 'rudiments' book. For *modulation*, see Ottó Károlyi, 1965, pp. 81–3.

The *autograph* or fully written-out version probably started off as a fair copy but Beethoven found he had to make changes, working out a great deal as he went along. Basing the autograph on his continuity draft, he harmonized and scored the melodic material he had prepared. But in case he might want to change his mind about small detail, and would have to alter what he had put down, the autograph was always written with very large bars, allowing plenty of room for second thoughts to be accommodated conveniently in the appropriate places. In the autograph of a symphony, for example, he would often have only three bars to a page, and as the score was intended to be read by other musicians, a music publisher, for example, or a copyist, it was written out in the conventional musical notation.

But Beethoven's handwriting, even when he had to try to be reasonably legible, is not easy for one who is not used to reading it. To prevent errors going into the printed edition, therefore, through misunderstandings on the engraver's part, the composer's autograph score was normally copied out by a professional copyist who was familiar with Beethoven's handwriting and who knew how to set out the score in the clearest possible manner for the engraver. With early works Beethoven had been in the practice of sending his autograph score to the publisher, but from about 1804 or '5 a professionally prepared copy was generally made for the publisher's use – legibility of handwriting being a major reason for the change!

You may care to look now at the illustrations on pages 51–2, which you can see are stages in the composition of the *Piano Trio in D major, op. 70 no. 1.*

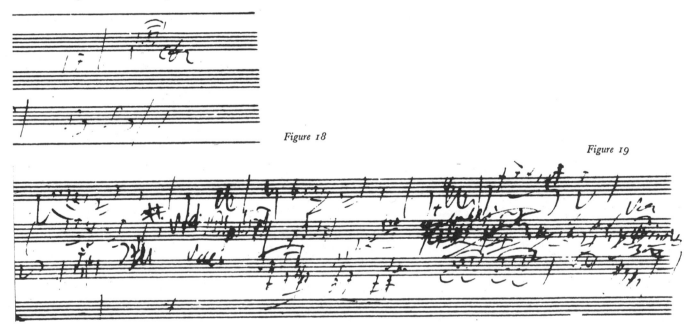

Figure 18

Figure 19

In Figure 18 you can see one of the first ideas Beethoven noted down for this slow movement. It was written in his desk-sized sketch-book. If he noted it previously in a pocket book it has since been lost. Already in the generative idea shown here Beethoven has two of the elements which are to hold the stage for the greater part of the movement: the slow-moving crotchets describing a curve upward (the small step down and a leap up) and that energetic rhythmic figure. But, you'll note, no key signature or time signature, and the treble clef sign is omitted.

Beethoven then tried to write the main melodic line straight off, correcting himself as he went along but did not get further than the eleventh bar. Perhaps he decided to make short work of it by starting on the autograph, or it is more

Figures 18–19 From a musical sketch-book of Ludwig van Beethoven, MSS Add. 31766 (British Museum) 18: sketch 52v; 19: sketch 53r.

Figure 20 Beethoven, sketches of op. 70 no. 1, page 16 (Mary Flagler-Cary Music Collection, Pierpont Morgan Library, New York).

probable that he had been disturbed at that point, and when he resumed sketching out the main melodic line he did so on another sheet of paper which has since been lost. You can see the sketch, with all the elements compressed on one line, in Figure 19. Again the handwriting is very untidy and Beethoven did not bother to use some of the conventional aids of notation. Even those he does use are haphazard; the imprecise rhythmic notation of bar 6, for example, and the way that he does not have all the bars of regular length. There is no indication of the harmony, and there is only a suggestion of the contrapuntal movement.

It is possible that when he wrote out the autograph Beethoven made such a mess of the first few pages of this movement that a copyist had to decipher them and make a clean copy before anyone else could make any sense out of them. The remainder of the movement is in Beethoven's hand, and Figure 20 gives you a glimpse of him changing his mind – he wrote the one version out, didn't like it, scrubbed it out, and substituted a second way of doing it.

EXERCISE

In 1813 Beethoven wrote in reply to George Thomson, the Scottish music publisher, who had requested him to modify some of the arrangements of national songs Beethoven had been making: 'I am not accustomed to revising my compositions; I have never done so, because I am convinced of the truth that every slight change alters the character of the whole composition.' (*Selected letters of Beethoven*, p. 126 – in French.)

1 How can what Beethoven says here be consistent with what he did in the normal process of composition?

2 You know, however, of one of his greatest works which he did revise considerably. Which was it?

Do this before going on

ANSWERS

1 Beethoven refused to change something which, after a lot of revising he regarded as his *final version*. To change that would only be to weaken it in his view, or to replace it by something pointlessly different. (Thomson was not satisfied, not because the music was not beautiful but because Beethoven's accompaniments were too difficult, 'in this country there is not one pianist in a hundred who can . . . play four notes in one hand and three in the other.' – Thomson's letter of 5 August 1812, quoted in Pamela J. Willetts, *Beethoven and England*, London, British Museum, 1970, p. 19.) To have altered an introduction or a particular part of the accompaniment would have meant reworking the whole song again. What he says here is consistent with his usual practice: once it had reached the printer's copy stage, he had finished the composition and did not alter it afterwards.

2 The opera, *Fidelio*. Here, however, the design of the work as a whole – something that the librettist and the producer had control over as well as the composer – was greatly altered: three acts become two, etc. So Beethoven's contribution had to be recast too, much as he objected to doing so (see *Selected letters of Beethoven*, p. 133).

SECTION 3 LISTENING TO BEETHOVEN'S MUSIC – WITH EMPHASIS ON TECHNICAL DETAIL

Introduction

Figure 21 Beethoven's study in the Schwarzspanierhaus, lithograph from a drawing by Johann Nepomuk Hoechle, 7 April 1827 (Museum der Stadt Wien).

These three Beethoven units fall more or less equally into a *reading* half and a *listening* half.

If you have read Sections 1 and 2 attentively you will, by now, have formed a picture of Beethoven the professional musician. In Dr Tyson's radio talk, particularly, and to a lesser extent in the foregoing sections, Beethoven's rôle as an artist of revolutionary importance has been outlined. Your conception of how significant a figure he was will, I believe, be strengthened the more you read *Beethoven, Impressions by his Contemporaries.*

We come now to the *listening* part of these units in which we pay attention to the music rather than to the composer. In Sections 3 and 4 you are asked to consider certain aspects of Beethoven's music. In the accompanying radio talks Professor Joseph Kerman discusses the revolutionary nature of Beethoven's music and the strength of his influence on succeeding generations of composers. The radio talks are the most appropriate place to deal with these crucial matters. We can play for you in these programmes the relevant music, so that you can hear for yourself how Beethoven's music *was* different from his contemporaries', and was in so many ways to have an effect on nineteenth-century music (if in some ways a negative as well as a positive one).

Through listening seriously to the music on the two gramophone records provided and in the Beethoven programmes on radio and television, it should be possible for you to gain a fairly reliable impression of the characteristics of Beethoven's style.

But what does 'listening to music' involve? My response to a piece of music is both cognitive and emotional. I can measure my ability to perceive what Beethoven does, for instance, in using a particular rhythmic figure, or in changing the harmonic accompaniment to a melody, altering the orchestration of a passage, and so on. But how should I gauge my emotional response? If I could, would it really help you if I told you about it? You may be moved emotionally by quite different musical effects from me, and there is no criterion for judging which, if either of us, has the 'right' emotional response. Or, I may not make any emotional response at all – in which case words describing someone else's response to the music will remain as words only, they won't create the same experience for me.

In everyday conversation one may attribute emotional qualities to music, assuming that the person being spoken to has an idea what is meant. But it is doubtful whether there is any value to such an approach in discussing Beethoven's music by correspondence. In the sections which follow, dealing with the music, I am therefore making a distinction between cognition and emotion in our experience of the pieces discussed.

In Section 3 my aim is to make you aware of certain characteristics in Beethoven's music. Equally, I shall draw your attention to the kind of features you should be taking notice of while listening to *any* piece of music – the main rhythmic elements; the shape and length of phrases in the melody; the harmony; the choice of instruments and the way that these are deployed in order to create a particular texture of sound; the proportions of the movement, and the possible relationship of one section with another, and so on.

In Section 4 I am asking you to think about how the music affects you emotionally. In asking you to listen to music composed at different periods of Beethoven's life, I hope you will recognize certain differences in the character of the music. I'll pose few questions and give fewer answers.

What I hope you will do is spend a lot of time listening to the records, becoming aware of as much detail as possible of what is being done in the music technically, while 'opening' yourself to *experience* the music. I suggested, in referring to Beethoven's middle-period music, on page 36, it was a measure of his stature that the majority of the works listed are still played today, most of them as often as any composition of the same genre by any other composer. This could be said for his late works as well. Beethoven's output was not, perhaps, as large as that of many of his contemporaries, including Haydn and Mozart, but it was a particularly rich one. The music I have chosen for discussion in the following section, though illustrating a number of genres and musical forms, isn't entirely representative. We don't have time for more than a preliminary inspection of a very small amount of Beethoven's music. In their own way all of the pieces chosen are outstanding, but such a selection is bound to be a personal one, and with a composer whose output is as rich as Beethoven's there could be very many different choices, equally rewarding for discussion. I hope you will enjoy mine.

Your becoming familiar with the pieces on record will probably add depth to your acquaintance with Beethoven as gained through the biographical sketch and *Beethoven, Impressions by his Contemporaries*. Certainly the discipline of listening carefully, in order to answer questions on these particular pieces, can be useful in making you *more aware* when you listen to any music at all. The score is provided of certain movements. If you need to improve your ability to read music notation, perhaps you'd care to follow the score with the record.

The disadvantage in making a selection of movements from different works, as on our gramophone records, is that in listening to them one is not aware of the context in which the movements selected occur. Close analysis often reveals the painstaking concern Beethoven had for finding the appropriate environment for his ideas: not only within the structure of a particular kind of movement but with the whole work in mind as well. In taking only an excerpt, as we do, from *Symphony No. 1* we have sacrificed a knowledge of even the structural context for the sake of receiving a fleeting impression, at least, of Beethoven's early instrumental writing. We do have a complete movement, however, from the *Piano Sonata op. 2 no. 3* to illustrate Beethoven's sense of form during the early period. Most record space is given to music of the middle period. In the late period, you will recall, Beethoven composed far fewer works (though those included some of his very finest music) but they were often on such an immense scale that we are up against the problem of whether we lose more than we gain by taking excerpts out of context.

Here are the movements in the order in which we shall be referring to them.

(i)   Overture *Egmont* op. 84. Complete.

(ii)   *Piano Trio in D major, op. 70 no. 1 'The Ghost'* The second movement, *Largo assai ed espressivo.*

(iii)   *Symphony no. 1 in C major, op. 21* An excerpt from the third movement, Minuet *Allegro molto e vivace.*

(iv)   *Piano sonata in F minor, op. 57*, the *Appassionata.* The first movement, *Allegro assai.*

(v)   *Violin concerto in D major, op. 61.* The last movement, *Rondo.*

(vi)   *Piano Sonata in C major, op. 2 no. 3.* The first movement, *Allegro con brio.*

(vii)   *String quartet in E flat major,* op. 127. Finale.

(viii) *'O welche Lust, in freier Luft'* from *Fidelio.*

(i) Overture *Egmont, op. 84*

Play the overture through. It is on the FIRST BEETHOVEN RECORD side 1 band 1.

Do this before going on

Even if you are 'coming in cold' to this, without knowing anything at all about it, you would probably find it a forceful, very exciting piece of music. Beethoven composed it as part of some incidental music in response to a commission by the Vienna Burgtheater in 1809, for a revival of a play by Goethe in 1810. Writing about the overture in a BBC Music Guide, Roger Fiske says:

> When [Beethoven] thought the music was about to be published, he wrote to Goethe, whom he had not then met, and promised him a copy, paying tribute to 'that glorious Egmont on which I have again reflected through you, and which I have reproduced in music as intense as my feelings when I read your play'. The subject was very close to his heart.[1]
>
> Count Egmont was a sixteenth-century Netherlander who resisted Spanish oppression of his country under the Duke of Alba. Despite his efforts to mediate between the Duke and the Calvinist hotheads of his own land, he was imprisoned by Alba and executed. In Goethe's tragedy Clärchen, who loves Egmont, foresees the execution and poisons herself. Egmont, sleeping in his cell, has a vision of Freedom (with Clärchen's features) who holds the victor's wreath above his head. While he is being led to execution, the orchestra plays what Goethe calls a 'victory symphony'.
>
> (R. Fiske, *Beethoven Concertos and Overtures*, BBC Publications, 1970, p. 57.)

EXERCISE

1 What technical means does Beethoven use to impart what I've called a forceful character to this piece?

2 The overture starts in a slow tempo, but it does not continue right through like this. How many changes of tempo are there?
Make a diagram to represent approximately the proportionate length of playing time in each tempo. You might make a note of the actual length of each section.
Play the overture through again.

Do this before going on

SPECIMEN ANSWER

1 An impression of sheer force is given right at the outset with the loud orchestral unison. The rhythm of the opening figure is marked and precise; there is a persistent repetition of part of this figure throughout most of the slow section, and in the succeeding fast section this same clipped rhythmic figure is heard again. Beethoven makes much use of short melodic, rhythmic figures which by continuous repetition work up an urgent feeling of drive. Although most of the melodic material consists of short fragments, when we hear a longer melody (after the slow opening when we have just gone into the fast section) this theme has a wide range extending over two octaves. It is not cramped and nervous; its lack of rhythmic fussiness – the first phrase is simply a succession of eleven crotchets – and its wide range, are

[1]It certainly was. It is relevant that Vienna was bombarded and invaded by the French in May 1809, and that Beethoven should take up this theme with relish and interest in the autumn following.

confident. The harmonic texture is generally full and, particularly towards the end in the extended passages for full orchestra, the build-up to a very loud level of sound produces, again, a powerful effect.

	2·25	4·25	1·25
2 Three:	slow	fast	even faster

DISCUSSION

You may have noticed before, in listening to a symphony or a sonata, for example, that the successive movements are often of a different character from one another. Contrast in tempi is a means of underlining these differences, though one doesn't need to have listened to much music to know that tempo and character cannot be simply equated. There would be little value in the generalization that, for instance, 'happy' music is fast and 'sad' music slow, because the opposite is also often the case and, anyway, one does not always feel that music has any distinctive emotional character as such. When one *can* recognize a definable character, through a particular emotional response to it perhaps, one might try to decide how the composer created it. How has he used the musical elements? The rhythmic element is often strongly in evidence if you feel the music has a distinctive character. It is here, in *Egmont*. But in considering also the kind of melodies used, the harmony and the way this is spaced out and shared amongst the instruments involved in the composition, one sees that it must be the interrelationship of all these elements which makes a good piece of music uniquely satisfying. In mentioning, therefore, the persistent repetition of the rhythmic figure in the slow introduction as a means of giving the overture the powerful character it has, we should go on to say this is so only because the rhythmic element is carried by appropriate melodic and harmonic elements at a convincing level of loudness or softness.

You read in the quotation above about the music Goethe calls a 'victory symphony'. Beethoven found it entirely appropriate to the formal structure of the overture to use the music he had composed as a 'victory symphony' in the play, to bring the overture itself to a close. Some people feel that in the overture Beethoven foreshadows emotionally the development in the tragedy.

If you have not identified the third section yet, when you listen to the overture next, note that to both the slow introduction and the subsequent main body of the overture, which is fast, you can count three beats in a bar (three very slow beats in the introduction). But after a big build-up, ending with an alternation between wind instruments (playing loudly) and the strings (playing softly), there is a dramatic pause. Wind instruments play some quiet chords, then the final section starts immediately. The music is now in a new metre: you can only count a quick two in a bar. There is more activity, and you might have thought the music sounded somehow brighter and grander. This may be partly on account of Beethoven's choice of orchestration (the violins and flute play particularly high and the piccolo has been added) and also, the music has changed into the major from the minor key.

The following exercise is meant to be helpful for less experienced listeners. Practising musicians and regular concert-goers will find they won't need to spend time on it. Simply, it is to check that the sounds of the different orchestral instruments are recognized.

EXERCISE

Listen to the overture *Egmont* again and fill in the missing words: to help draw attention to the features you are asked to identify, you'll hear them referred to by number.

After the opening orchestral unison the . . . . (1) (wind, brass, percussion, strings?) play for three bars, ending quietly. The following wind instruments are then heard entering one by one to build up a quiet chord: first the . . . . (2), then the . . . . (3) and the . . . . (4). The same melodic figure is taken up quietly by the strings only to cadence on to a loud orchestral unison, which we recognize as identical with the one we heard at the very beginning. The full orchestra then plays the strong rhythmic figure of the opening . . . . (5) (once, twice, three times?), the . . . . (6) (wind, brass, percussion, string?) section recall the quiet melodic figure previously used to build up to a wind chord and a string passage, and the music then seems to settle down to a more straightforward tune-and-accompaniment kind of writing.

We hear the violins play the first phrase of the tune. This is repeated but with a slightly different orchestral colour; the violin melody is doubled (i.e. another instrument is playing the same phrase as well) by a . . . . (7). The following phrase is doubled by a . . . . (8), which also is joined in the next repetition of the phrase by a . . . . (9). The Allegro begins seven bars later with a scurrying figure on the strings, quickly subsiding into an accompaniment as the first theme of the Allegro is heard on the . . . . (10). After a short build-up to a loud climax we hear this theme again on the . . . . (11).

Do this before going on

I know that as the music continues, it is only too easy to be left behind on this exercise unless you are quick. If you found it difficult to identify what I was referring to, listen again, this time following the diagrammatic 'chart' of the section which is on page 59. This is not a standard form of notation but a simple visual aid[1] to perceiving more of what is taking place in the music. Count steadily as indicated and you won't lose your place. The features referred to are identified by number on the chart as well as on the record (up to 10).

[1] I am indebted for this to Donald Burrows, Staff Tutor in Music at the Open University.

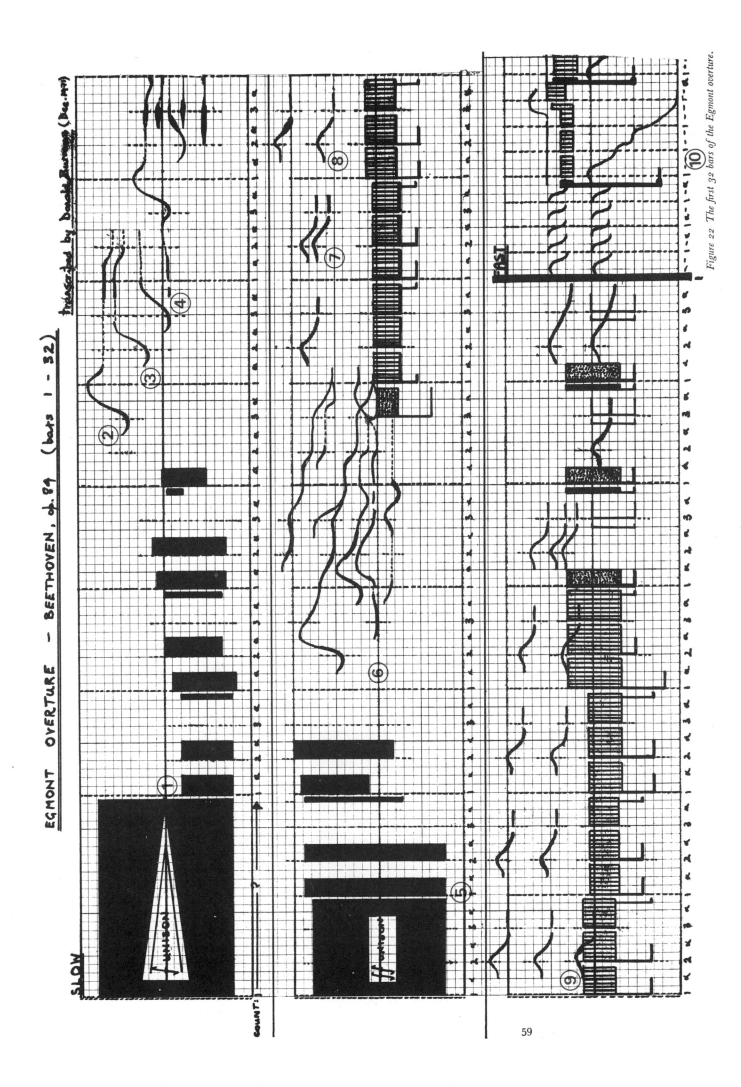

Figure 22 The first 32 bars of the Egmont overture.

ANSWERS

1   Strings
2   Oboe
3   Clarinet
4   Two bassoons
5   Twice
6   Wind
7   Clarinet
8   Flute
9   Bassoon
10 Cellos
11 Violins

COMMENT

If you found, on taking this opportunity to check your ability to recognize the sounds of different instruments, that you did not do so well, you might, as an emergency measure, go to your study centre and look at Film No. A.100 14, *Instruments of the Orchestra*. This ought to help you place the distinctions between the tone quality of one instrument and another, and enable you to continue working through these units with a better grasp of what I'm referring to. Looking ahead, it is worth learning what all the instruments look like[1] so that when you have seen them play in an orchestra, it will be easier to remember the kind of sound they make.

Turn now to the score of this section of the overture *Egmont*, which is on pages 61–2. The features you have identified aurally are again referred to by number on the score.

You may never have followed a score in musical notation before, even so you will notice that the visual impression of the lines traced out by the notes in each instrument's part is not unsimilar to the blocks and wavy lines on the much simpler 'chart' of the music. One would not wish to take this comparison much further because in reading an orchestral score we have the added complication of having to make a mental adjustment in imagining the sound of instruments whose parts are *transposed*. (Simply: all is not what it might appear to be! For reasons mainly to do with technical facility in playing the part the sound of the notes played may actually be higher or lower than you'd expect from what is written.)

Play this section of the overture, following the score as you listen.

Do this before going on

---

[1] If you cannot go to a musical instrument shop to see the instruments themselves, any illustrated dictionary, or Units 13 and 14 of the Arts Foundation Course, *Introduction to Music*, would be useful. Blind students would find helpful the gramophone record, 'Sir Adrian Boult introduces the Instruments of the Orchestra' (Music for Pleasure, MFP.2092).

Egmont

Overture

L. van BEETHOVEN, Op. 84

Sostenuto ma non troppo

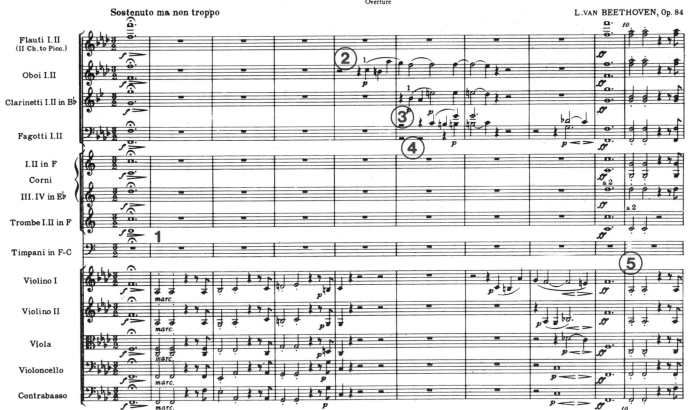

(ii) *Piano Trio in D major, op. 70 no. 1 ('The Ghost')*
Largo assai ed espressivo

Beethoven's op. 1, the music he chose to launch himself in Vienna as a *composer*, was a set of piano trios. He had plumped for a genre he could tackle well, and there was also the obvious advantage of his being able to perform in the piano trio himself at the musical soirées of his aristocratic admirers. That the piano part had been regarded at the end of the eighteenth century as the leading part in chamber music with piano, may be seen from the title pages of compositions by Haydn, Mozart and their contemporaries: violin sonatas, for example – 'sonata for pianoforte with violin accompaniment' – and piano trios – 'sonata for pianoforte, with an accompaniment for a violin and a violoncello'. This began to change in the first ten years of the nineteenth century until by now we have become accustomed to thinking of the piano as an *accompaniment* instrument in so much music. The original form of these titles consequently seems odd to us. If you listen very carefully to the movement we are discussing, you may feel that the violin part *is* marginally less rewarding than the cello's, and both less rewarding than the piano's.

The two piano trios op. 70 were dedicated to Countess Anna Marie Erdödy (1779–1837), a great admirer of Beethoven's music and, at the time of their composition possibly the object of his affections as well. She was a fine pianist, and patron whose support and influence was felt through the concerts she held at her home. The trios were composed in 1808, in the same year as the *Pastoral Symphony* (Symphony no. 6 in F major, op. 68) the sketches for both being in the same sketch-book, which is now in the British Museum. You have already seen extracts from this sketch-book illustrating Section 2, on Beethoven's process of composition, on page 51.

EXERCISE
Listen to the beginning of the movement which is on the FIRST BEETHOVEN RECORD, side 1 band 2. The music starts quietly but after about a minute and a half reaches a loud climax in which the piano is particularly noticeable. Immediately after that the music becomes suddenly quiet, and you hear a slowly descending passage covering two octaves on the piano. What happens then? (This time, listen, don't look at the score.)

Do this before going on

ANSWER
The melodic material from the very beginning returns, but now with a tremolo accompaniment on the piano.

COMMENT
When I listen to this, I am excited by the change and by what Beethoven does. Although he starts it quietly, this tremolo is a very potent means of creating excitement later as the music builds up to a climax. It was this effect in the accompaniment, incidentally, which was considered so eerie in the nineteenth century as to warrant nicknaming it '*The Ghost*' trio.

You will find a reference, on pages 51 and 52 of *Beethoven, Impressions by his Contemporaries*, to a composition which might have influenced Beethoven in the use of the tremolo. The event described took place in about 1797.

When listening to the slow movement of Beethoven's *Piano Trio in D major, op. 70 no. 1* you will notice how persistent use is made of certain material. It is a fairly long movement yet, because it is so economically written, it is not too difficult to identify the main material and to observe what changes it undergoes.

EXERCISE

Taking the foregoing exercise as an instance of the kind of thing you might listen for, make a note of what strikes you as the most significant melodic and rhythmic material. Identify these elements, and comment as fully as you can on the way Beethoven integrates and modifies them in the course of the movement.

We are usually more aware visually than aurally, so I would suggest you try doing this exercise by listening only, to begin with. But if you can read music notation, refer to the score, which is on pages 64–9 to see if you can add anything to your answer afterwards. Play the FIRST BEETHOVEN RECORD side 1 band 2.

Do this before going on

I'm not giving an answer to this exercise here. There is *one* television component in the three-week Beethoven block, a programme which deals entirely with the subject of this exercise.

The programme presents my view of the slow movement of Beethoven's *Piano Trio in D major, op. 70 no. 1*. It is a critical analysis of it – you will hear the separate elements of the music played and see how they are integrated. You should make every effort to come to your own conclusions before watching the programme, because it gives the full answer to the exercise. I have treated this as central to the teaching of these units.

66

In presenting my view of the movement I refer to Beethoven's sketches as well as the final version, and by directing your attention to a particular member of the trio at a certain moment, and repeating this a number of times, hope to give *visual emphasis* to the musical points I want to make. Going back to the gramophone record, it is hoped that you might listen at a more complex level, and be able to extend this practice to other music as well.

If you are in the mood for this music, you'll respond to its appeal. I chose to examine it in detail partly because it is a work for which the full series of sketches is still extant (the sketch-book in the British Museum and the autograph in the Pierpont Morgan Library, New York) and, more important, because it exemplifies the more striking characteristics of Beethoven's style in the middle period: its great intensity in particular, the concentration of material and the assurance with which it is handled.

(iii)   *Symphony No. 1 in C Major, op. 21*
        Minuet, Allegro molto e vivace

To feel the contrast between the mature style of Beethoven's work in 1808, and that of ten years earlier, listen now to the excerpt taken from this instrumental composition of the early period.

Play the FIRST BEETHOVEN RECORD side 1 band 3.

Do this before going on

EXERCISE

Jot down what impressions you have of the difference between the style of *Egmont* and *Piano Trio op. 70 no. 1* and of this excerpt from the *First Symphony*. The question is about style, *not* differences of genre.

Do this before going on

ANSWER

Although this movement of the symphony seemed to be getting on with something vigorously, in a confident manner, it might possibly be felt to be a more 'open' confidence than that recognized in the later works, with the result that you responded differently to it. You probably didn't even think of confidence in *Egmont* and 'The Ghost'; this quality is so strong that I, for one, accept the total authority of the composer in the music and it doesn't occur to me to make a complimentary observation like admiring his confidence. This is the mature Beethoven, *of course* he writes with authority!

COMMENT

Every now and again one needs reminding of the obvious fact that since Beethoven's time a great deal of music has been written and, less obvious perhaps, that the whole climate of musical appreciation has changed radically.

Those of you who took the Arts Foundation Course will remember that we looked at this change in the Mendelssohn units (Units 27 and 28). Very briefly, what happened? Up to Beethoven's time music had been, to varying degrees of exclusiveness, something pursued for the enjoyment of the educated classes, and the popular taste was invariably for contemporary music. Towards the end of the eighteenth century, when the Baroque style had been superseded by what became technically a more difficult style of music to play, signs of nostalgia for non-contemporary music could be seen amongst amateurs who met to play programmes of what they called 'ancient music'. They were a very small minority. Most people for whom music was part of their lives continued in the traditional manner to regard what was new as the essential current repertoire, and to discard the old, used music. This partly accounts for the high number of works Haydn wrote, for example: at least 104 symphonies, something like 80 string quartets, 20 operas, and so on. As he continued to write new works, the earlier ones tended naturally to drop out of use to make room for them in the limited amount of concert playing-time there was. A few musicians were not so hypnotized by the continuing attraction of newly-composed music as to be blind to the beauty of earlier compositions from those of J. S. Bach back to Palestrina in the sixteenth century, and very gradually it became more generally appreciated what a great store there was of music worth resuscitating.

In our musical case study in the Foundation Course, we underlined the significance, as part of this movement, of Mendelssohn's revival of Bach's *St Matthew Passion*.

You read how in time it became popularly acceptable to have music of other periods alongside contemporary music in concert programmes. Public taste in music, from being exclusively restricted to the latest in the contemporary style, became more catholic.

Figure 23 Cover of A100 Units 27 and 28, Mendelssohn's Rediscovery of Bach.

We may *now* derive as much pleasure listening to a fifteenth-century French *chanson* as a composition by one of today's *avant garde*, or any piece of music in the styles which come in between these extremes. We don't confine ourselves to the music of our own culture either. Recitals of African and Eastern music are not infrequently broadcast in this country, and the influence of Indian and Japanese music, in particular, is being felt in Western contemporary music. Such a variety of music is so easily available that, paradoxically, many people are confused by the choice, and find themselves falling back on to the inert assurance of, 'I know what I like, and like what I know.' The most familiar today is not the music of living composers but the great corpus of the nineteenth-century Romantics. We are used to the degree of emotional involvement their music often calls for, and the experienced listener, who is familiar with the wide range of current styles, doesn't get easily shocked. As our own musical environment is so rich, it is not easy to imagine what it must have been like to have been a listener at a concert of Beethoven's music a century and a half ago. And because of the way our own experience of music has been conditioned, it is impossible for us to feel the forceful impact of his music precisely as his contemporaries did.

You have listened to the overture *Egmont*. This is a composition which, despite everything that has happened between then and now, we still feel has something urgent and forceful about it. (If you disagree, I would encourage you first to see whether you are giving the music a chance by playing it on a reasonable record player, or, go to a good live performance of the overture, where the effect I am talking about is most likely to be experienced.) *Symphony No. 5* is another such piece you may be familiar with. In Beethoven's time people found some of his music painfully exhilarating to listen to. When we think about works like *Egmont* or *Symphony No. 5* we may believe this, but the fact was that even his early compositions, which may sound innocent enough to us took his contemporaries by surprise.

Remember that Mendelssohn's revival performances of the Bach *St Matthew Passion* took place two years to the month after Beethoven had died. For the length of his career Beethoven was producing music for audiences whose taste was for *new* music.[1] They had not yet been educated to appreciate anything older than the contemporary. Even so, in Beethoven they sometimes found too strongly in evidence what Goethe called his 'utterly untamed personality' (*Beethoven, Impressions by his Contemporaries*, p. 88).

There is a danger that in studying Beethoven today we forget how the musical background of the cultured people for whom Beethoven improvised at the piano, and who first heard his quartets and symphonies, was very different from our own. And there is a danger (which I recognize as being particularly near in a course of this nature) that although we find out a great deal about him, and may speculate as to why he did certain things in the way he did, we might end up musically the poorer for having killed our own emotional response to Beethoven's music in straining to grasp too much too quickly. We all respond differently to Beethoven's appeal, and rather than cause you annoyance through subjecting you to a biased view of what kind of emotional response I might be having to the pieces discussed, I have refrained from giving much in this direction.

I have placed more emphasis on some aspects of analysis into which we will look further in our specialist music courses. Although you may be finding many of the exercises difficult, I hope you'll conclude, perhaps later, that analysis may deepen and affirm your response to a piece of music.

The experience is the essence of the music. The primary requisite is to 'open' yourself to the music, to have an experience to interpret.

You might, as a rule, reason that if an effect strikes you as surprising, it would probably have sounded even more so to someone listening in Beethoven's time. You have had many an indication already, in what you have read in these units, of the effect performances of Beethoven's music had at the time. Here is another comment, written in the 1830s by the Scotsman George Hogarth (1783–1870). He is not a significant musical historian, but, as one of the early musical journalists, is interesting, and his writing reflects popular opinions on music in the period immediately after Beethoven's death.

> His first publications were treated with great severity by the German journalists, by whom he was accused of harsh modulations, melodies more singular than pleasing, and a constant straining after originality. It is always the fate of genius, such as Beethoven's, to be censured before it is understood. Those productions, so roughly treated by the Aristarchs of the time, probably contained crudities to which youthful inexperience is liable; but they must have been much akin, in style and character, to those compositions which follow them very closely in point of date, and which form the commencement of the regular series of his published works. Now the very earliest of these, – his three trios for the pianoforte, violin, and violoncello; his sonatas, dedicated to Haydn, and his first trio for a violin, (viola), and violoncello, – are at present looked upon as correct, clear, and smooth compositions; yet, within our remembrance, these pieces were considered,

---

[1] Hence, incidentally, the popularity of the improvisation contests held at the musical soirées of the aristocracy.

in England, as wild, crabbed, and unintelligible. When his symphony in C minor [*the Fifth Symphony*] was first tried by the band of the Philharmonic Society, an assemblage of musical ability not surpassed in the world, they were so astounded at its odd and abrupt outset, and so bewildered by the novelty of its harmonies and transitions, that it was not till after several repetitions, that its amazing grandeur and beauty began to unfold themselves even to *their* enlightened vision.

(George Hogarth, *Musical History, Biography and Criticism*, London, John W. Parker, 1838, Vol. 2, p. 124.)

Returning to the excerpt from the *First Symphony*: here is another exercise which suggests the kind of detail one listens for in any piece of music (FIRST BEETHOVEN RECORD, side 1 band 3).

EXERCISE

1 Beethoven keeps a certain rhythm going throughout most of the excerpt on the record. You might try tapping it out with the music, then make a note of the pattern. Devise your own way of noting it or choose which it is of the following:
   (a) Strong – weak – strong – weak – strong – weak, *etc.*
   (b) Strong – weak – weak – strong – weak – weak, *etc.*
   (c) Strong – weak – weak – weak – weak – weak – Strong – weak – weak – weak – weak – weak, *etc.*
   (d) STRONG – weak – strong – STRONG – weak – strong, *etc.*
   (e) STRONG – weak – strong – weak – STRONG – weak – strong – weak, *etc.*

2 Describe the melodic contour of the opening. You notice that this is repeated immediately. How many phrases are there, and do you think these complement each other in any way?

3 Where, do you feel, does the climax of the opening section come? (This is the section which is repeated immediately, so the climax comes in the same position twice.)

4 After the repeat of the first section, we hear fresh material. Shortly, the music settles on a long held note in the bass above which the strings alternate with woodwind, playing a short phrase in imitation. The following passage is obviously preparing us for something more significant to come. Describe what comes.

5 The second section is also repeated, then the music takes on a more gentle lilt. This is the beginning of the Trio. Which of the rhythmic patterns listed in question 1 is it which you hear recurring in this new section?

6 Which section of the orchestra plays the repeated rhythmic, chordal figure?

7 Which instruments interpolate with lithe melodic phrases?

8 From your experience of listening to symphonies, from which of the conventional order of four movements in a symphony is this music taken, do you think?

Do this before going on

ANSWERS

1 The recurring rhythmic pattern is (d):
   (Strong) – STRONG – weak – strong – STRONG – weak – strong *etc.*

2 It is an ascending passage following the steps of the scale extending over a range of an octave and a half and finally dropping down a fifth. Two phrases. The second echoes, but not exactly, the shape of the first. The same rhythm is kept going through both, and the effect, from the beginning of the

first phrase to the end of the second, is that the music is fanning out in pitch as the melody rises and the bass extends downward.

3   At the very end.

4   The opening material again, which seems heavier and we notice the addition of a stabbing trumpet figure, which adds impetus to the urgent onward drive of the music.

5   Same as 1, but without the upbeat: STRONG – weak – strong – STRONG – weak – strong – *etc*.

6   The woodwind.

7   Violins.

8   The rhythm, in particular, and the short decisive shape of the phrases give the clue. It is the third movement; Beethoven is giving us a very vigorous form of the traditional *Minuet* and Trio. Although it is entitled a Minuet, this is typical of the energetic kind of movement subsequently to be called a *Scherzo* which Beethoven was to write in place of the Minuet within the structure of his symphonies and string quartets.

The criticism levelled against the symphony on its first performance, on 2 April 1800 is of relevance here. The reviewer for the *Allgemeine Musikalische Zeitung* of Leipzig found that the symphony, 'contained much artistry, novelty, and richness of ideas; the only objection was that the wind instruments were employed excessively, so that it was more military band than orchestral music' (Schmidt-Görg and Schmidt, 1970, p. 35). This reminds us again to try to get the music into perspective, and to realize what an impact it would have made on Beethoven's listeners in the early years of the nineteenth century. The exciting wind writing we have become used to hearing, in later nineteenth- and twentieth-century orchestral works, has blunted the effect of Beethoven's orchestration on us.

(iv)   *Piano Sonata in F Minor, op. 57, the Appassionata*
        Allegro assai

In contrast, both of medium and style, would you now listen to the first movement of Beethoven's *Piano Sonata in F minor, op. 57*, the *Appassionata*, which is on the SECOND BEETHOVEN RECORD side 1 band 1, and make a note of your answers to the following exercise. Again, you are asked to listen for certain details, the kind of things you might be aware of when listening to any music.

EXERCISE

1   (a)   What is the tempo?
    (b)   How many beats are there in a bar?

2   Right at the beginning you hear a melodic phrase, then there is a very short silence before a second phrase is heard. Describe
    (a)   the shape of the melody
    (b)   its range
    (c)   rhythmic energy
    (d)   sonority
    (e)   the relationship of melody and harmony.

Do this before going on

ANSWER

1 (a) The music moves along at a rather fast pace, and you might therefore have put down *allegro*. Beethoven in fact qualifies it and heads the movement *allegro assai* (quite quick or pretty quick).

(b) Four beats.

2 (a) The obvious thing is that it makes a short dip down and a long sweep up (ending in fact an octave higher than it began). Most of the first three bars are taken up with notes on the main chord (called the tonic triad) in the key of F minor. The cadence figure contrasts with this in being concentrated around the dominant note, on which it ends. Here movement is by small, close steps.

(b) Its range is wide: from the low, bass notes of the opening – both hands are playing the same melody only they are doing so two octaves apart – to the highest note of the phrase.

(c) The harmony is simply the tonic chord for most of the first three bars. Played as elements of a triad without rhythmic shape these notes would have no force at all, but Beethoven has asserted a very tense, energetic rhythm which imparts to the music a sense of direction.

(d) The sound of the melody played in both hands two octaves apart, is rich, the upper part reinforcing the harmonics of the lower. After the melody describing the notes of tonic chord has risen to its upper limit, the colour changes as the right hand assumes the melodic interest and the left hand plays chords.

(e) Though the opening part of the phrase is played in both hands, and there is no distinct accompaniment to it, the harmony is clear – every note being part of the one chord. The last part of the phrase, in contrast, has the harmony stated as an accompaniment to the right-hand melody, which accentuates its inconclusiveness of cadence.

If you managed this exercise, and were aware of the points to which I was drawing your attention, try the one which follows. It is rather more difficult.

EXERCISE

Listen to the first minute of this movement only and make a note of your answers to the following.

1 You will recall that in describing the opening of the *Minuet* of Beethoven's *Symphony No. 1 in C major* (on p. 73), I drew your attention to the way the range of the music was extended both upward and downward. What is gradually happening in terms of pitch, in the first minute of the *Appassionata*?

2 How much use is made of the material of the opening phrase within the first minute of the movement?

3 How many times does a recognizable version of the whole phrase appear?

4 The second phrase is not quite the same as the first. What is the difference?

5 Two repetitions of the opening phrase lead on shortly to a pause on a quiet, low chord (following a dramatic build-up to a short, 'aggressive' downward sweep). Listen to the phrase immediately following the pause and say how it differs from the opening phrase of the movement.

6 The dynamic levels (i.e. whether the music is loud or soft) have an important function in this third repetition of the opening phrase. Can you say what it is?

Do this before going on

ANSWER

1 The music starts low, goes lower then rises. This establishes the 'pitch-zone' in which we are going to hear the action. From there on there is gradual concentration on the extreme limits of this zone and the music seems to be fanning out. Listen, for example, for this effect.

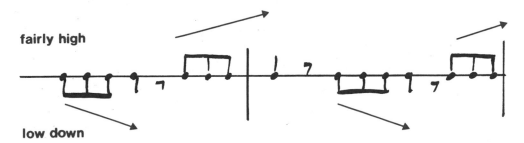

fairly high

low down

    This impression is strengthened by the vicious, mounting chords in the right hand, after the pause, which extend the upward limit of the zone of activity.

2 Most of the first minute is built on this material. After two statements of the opening phrase the tail end of it becomes detached. We hear it twice, with interventions, before the opening phrase is introduced again.

3 Three times.

4 It is in a different key. It starts a semitone higher than the first. You notice the change between the end of the first phrase and the beginning of the second. More than this, it is in a different *mode*: the opening is in the MINOR mode, but the second phrase is in the MAJOR.

5 The melody itself is the same, except that it has been interrupted three times – exploded into fragments, in between which a heavy, syncopated figure thrusts itself.

6 The contrasting dynamic levels help the ear differentiate between material of the melody and that of what has been inserted. The heavy vamp-like insertions are always *ff* (*fortissimo*, very loud) while the melody is very quiet (*pp*, *pianissimo*) as it was at the beginning.

Listen in particular now to the third statement of that phrase, the one which has been exploded into fragments, and note what form the interruptions take. If you can read music, this score, with the insertions left blank, may help you to see the complete line.

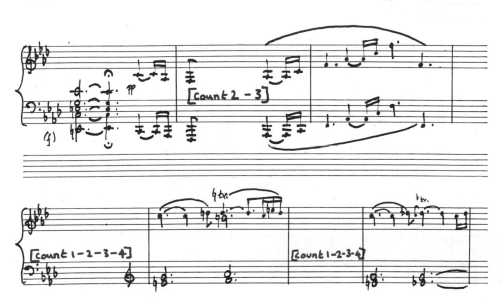

Each of the heavy intrusions is a very thick (i.e. containing many notes tightly placed under the fingers) statement of a single chord, in each case rising in syncopation with the bass. The intrusions create sudden *tension* because they are so unexpected, contrasting with the melody in loudness, texture and in rhythmic flow.

I have concentrated on a small amount of this piano sonata to draw attention to some details of the kind you might observe on listening to any music. An appreciation of what the composer has achieved technically may, though not invariably, add to one's satisfaction and pleasure in listening. I am certainly *not* saying that you can't enjoy listening to this sonata unless you are a pianist. That would be foolish. But I am sure that the more aware you are of all aspects of the music, the richer the experience of listening to it is likely to be for you. If you have found these exercises difficult, it is worth listening until you *do* observe the details mentioned. Hopefully, doing so will assist you to sharpen your musical perception in general.

The *Appassionata* was composed during 1804–6 and published the following spring. It was dedicated to Count Franz Brunswick, a close friend of Beethoven's, an admirer of his music and himself an amateur cellist. Beethoven was at that time deeply attached to one of the Count's sisters, Josephine Deym, who had been left a widow in 1804. Beethoven's hoped-for marriage did not materialize, and the cooling-off of the relationship may be seen from these extracts taken from letters separated in time by almost four years. One is a draft of a letter to Beethoven from Josephine, thought to have been written in the winter of 1804–5, and the other, the last surviving letter Beethoven wrote her, was probably the covering note sent with the published copy of the *Appassionata* for her brother.

1   My own spirit which, in any case, was *enthusiastic* for you even before I knew you, received nourishment from your inclination. A feeling which lies deep within my heart and is not capable of expression, made me love you. Before I met you your music made me *enthusiastic* for you – the goodness of your *character*, your inclination towards me increased my enthusiasm – this prerogative which you granted me, the pleasure of being with you, could have been the greatest jewel of my life if you loved me less sensually. Because I cannot satisfy this sensual love you are angry with me – I would have to destroy sacred bonds if I were to give heed to your desires. Believe me – that the fulfilment of my duties causes me the greatest suffering – and that surely the motives which guide my conduct are noble.

   (H. C. Robbins Landon, 1970, p. 194.)

2   Please deliver this sonata to your brother, my dear Josephine – I thank you for wishing still to appear as if I were not altogether banished from your memory, even though this came about perhaps more at the instigation of others – You want me to tell you how I am. A more difficult question could not be put to me – and I prefer to leave it unanswered, rather than – to answer it *too truthfully* – All good wishes, dear J.

                                             As always, your BEETHOVEN
                                             who is eternally devoted to you.

   (*Selected letters of Beethoven*, p. 79.)

(v)   *Violin Concerto in D major, op. 61*

Beethoven, you will remember, used to play the violin and viola as a young man at Bonn. But unlike Johann Sebastian Bach (1685–1750) whose fame as a virtuoso keyboard player had been almost matched by his ability to perform professionally as a violinist, Beethoven's writing for violin was influenced by what he learned from others, as much as by his own experience of the instrument.[1] *The Violin Concerto in D major, op. 61* was composed in 1806. By then he

[1] See what Beethoven's friend Ferdinand Ries had to say about his playing: *Beethoven, Impressions by his Contemporaries*, p. 58.

had gained considerable experience writing for the violin: in chamber and orchestral music in which the violin participated and, besides an early *Concerto in C major* for violin (of which only part of a movement has survived) and the two romances for violin and orchestra, Beethoven had quite recently completed his magnificent *Violin Sonata in A major, op. 47*, the *Kreutzer*. That was in 1803, the year of the *Eroica*. The brilliant, idiomatic writing of this sonata has the quality of a concerto about it, and this was deliberate. The first edition in fact makes a point of asserting that the sonata is 'written very much in a concertante style, almost like a concerto'.[1]

While Beethoven normally seemed to need months working on a composition before completing it, he succeeded in writing large-scale works very quickly indeed during two or three exceptional periods of activity. You have already read about *Christ on the Mount of Olives*, which was composed in little over a fortnight. The violin concerto was another work that was written very rapidly. It was ready only two days before its première on 23 December 1806 by the Viennese violinist, Franz Clement (1780–1842). Critical opinion, while noting that the audience had liked the concerto and particularly Clement's elegant performance, was not too encouraging.

> Musical authorities are unanimous in their opinion of Beethoven's Concerto: while they acknowledge that it contains some fine things, they agree that the continuity often seems to be completely disrupted, and that the endless repetitions of a few commonplace passages could easily lead to weariness. It is being said that Beethoven ought to make better use of his admittedly great talents, and give us works like his first Symphonies in C and D, his charming Septet in E flat, the spirited Quintet in D and others of his earlier compositions, which will assure him a permanent place among the foremost composers. It is feared, though, that if Beethoven continues to follow his present course, it will go ill both with him and the public. The music could soon fail to please anyone not completely familiar with the rules and difficulties of the art. Burdened by a host of unconnected and piled-up ideas, and continual tumult of different instruments which should merely create a characteristic effect at their entry, he could only leave the concert with an unpleasant sense of exhaustion.
>
> (Quoted from *Zeitung für Theater, Musik und Poesie*, Vienna, 8 January 1807 in Schmidt-Görg and Schmidt, 1970, pp. 53–4.)

The critic of the English musical journal *The Harmonicon* was even more disparaging, writing off the concerto, after the first London performance on 9 April 1832, as 'a *fiddling* affair' of the kind which 'might have been written by any third- or fourth-rate composer' (Willetts, 1970, p. 53).

This movement is a *Rondo*, a form so called because the tune we hear right at the beginning keeps coming round. In between statements of this are EPISODES of complementary material. As we become increasingly familiar with the main tune itself, in the course of the movement, we tend to look to the episodes for interest. Because the rondo tune is well defined, the contrasting sections of the movement are not difficult to identify.

Here is the rondo tune, which you hear right at the beginning of the movement played first by the solo violin twice, then the third time by the full orchestra (*tutti*).

[1]Beethoven, *Violin Concerto, Op. 61*, miniature score edition, Ernst Eulenburg Ltd. (No. 701) See Foreword.

The rondo form conveniently provides in its episodes an opportunity for the solo instrument to lead with interesting and attractive melodic material. See if you can identify the structural divisions of this movement now.

EXERCISE

Listen to the Rondo finale of Beethoven's *Violin Concerto, op. 61*. It is on the FIRST BEETHOVEN RECORD, side 2 band 1.

If we represent diagrammatically those sections in which the main tune is

heard (once or more) by ▬▬▬▬ and any other passages by a line ————,

draw a diagram to represent the structure of this movement. Let the diagram indicate the proportionate length of playing time of the various sections.

Do this before going on

ANSWER
See page 80.

EXERCISE

This is to draw your attention to points of orchestration in this Rondo. They are not, in this particular instance, features of revolutionary importance by any means. But, as in the programme on '*The Ghost*' trio, where I illustrated how Beethoven subtly altered the tone of certain passages through changing the instrumentation, I want *you* to observe one or two details.

1 The solo violin's first episode begins with the rhythm with which the full

orchestra had ended: ♪ | ♩ ♪ ♩ Immediately, the violin leaps to a very

high note. Name the instruments playing the accompaniment at that point. This is only a momentary colour: after an upward scale Beethoven repeats the violin phrase, with embellishment, and alters the instrumentation of the accompaniment. Which instruments play now?

Listen on through the movement. Note the bassoon solo during the second episode, a particularly lyrical line against which the violin solo weaves a counterpoint.

2 After the cadenza, which instruments enter first, while the violin holds a trill?

Listen for the exciting change in rhythmic accentuation, just before the end, when the full orchestra plays in syncopation against the natural metre, which we have become used to throughout the movement.

Listen to the FIRST BEETHOVEN RECORD, side 2 band 1.

Do this before going on

ANSWERS
1 The accompaniment is first played by two horns, then the same figure is taken by an oboe and a clarinet. You might also have noticed that the two bassoons and strings add a touch of colour at the end of each phrase.
2 The lowest instruments of the string section, cellos and double basses.

EXERCISE

This is to draw your attention to a melodic detail. Again, it is not a revolutionary point. Rather, this kind of thing happens in so much music that you might be aware of it and listen for it.

After the cadenza follows a passage leading to a trill on the solo violin, which then plays four slow, high notes before being joined by the orchestra again.

Identify this place by listening to the record.

If you have failed to find it after listening repeatedly, it might help to know it comes about three-quarters of a minute after the end of the cadenza (from when the cellos and double basses come in, after the violin solo).

Take note of the tune played by the wind section at the point where the orchestra join in after these four slow, high notes on the solo violin. It is the beginning of the rondo theme.

Can you identify what the solo violin then plays as a balancing phrase?
Listen to the FIRST BEETHOVEN RECORD, side 2 band 1.

Do this before going on

ANSWERS

The violin plays the rondo theme *upside down*. Because the rhythm continues as before you may feel the violin tune has a close affinity to the rondo theme. Now, instead of leaping from the first note of the rondo theme *down*, then *up*, the violin leaps *up* then *down*, and so on.

At the end of the eighteenth and beginning of the nineteenth century, music was composed in a dramatic style: certain techniques were used deliberately to disturb the listener. Of course, he liked being, and expected to be, disturbed in this way. In contrast with the music of the early eighteenth century (by Bach and Handel and their generation), in which the same emotional level was maintained fairly evenly right through a movement, the emotional level now fluctuated as the music rose to a climax, passed to a more tranquil passage, went on to the next section of conflict through to its resolution, and so on and on.

As this dramatic style was common language and all composers were concerned with the same kind of problem, it was natural that a common basis for solving it should evolve. What evolved, sonata form, differed from the earlier dance forms, in which the music had had to fit into a definite form (and the form was the same for all dances of the same kind by any composer) in that it was more a way of writing than a structure. It was the way of writing which Haydn, Mozart and Beethoven found most satisfying for what they had to say: they had found *it worked very well*. Mozart had been impressed by what Haydn did with it, and the older Haydn by what Mozart managed to achieve, and Beethoven by both. They could do great things in this form, and it was probably adopted by less gifted people than them because *they* found it an effective system to work by. If you took the Arts Foundation Course, you'll remember the description of sonata form given in Units 15 and 16, *Form and Meaning*, pages 22–5. A movement of a piano sonata of Haydn's was analysed and you were asked to identify elements used in a certain section.

I don't think a general course such as this is the place to go further into a detailed study of sonata form. But as most of the movements Beethoven wrote are in sonata form, I want to emphasize a single point here: although the more memorable aspect of a movement in the classical style may be the way in which themes complement each other in 'dialogue', the fundamental element contributing to the strength and interest of the structure *is the relationship of those keys in which the themes appear.* And it was in the choice of key relationships within the overall tonal structure of a movement that Beethoven extended the scope of sonata form in one way.

In the analysis programme on the slow movement of the *Piano Trio op. 70 no. 1,* I mentioned how a certain passage had a particularly striking effect, because it came in what wasn't conventionally considered to be the 'right' key. Because music was a common language people had certain expectations, such as that at the beginning of a movement there should be a modulation to the dominant which, established as a new tonal centre for an extended period, allowed a certain amount of tension to build up. When Beethoven didn't go to the dominant but gave an unexpected key the function normally performed by the dominant, the effect was striking not only on account of its being unconventional. The revolutionary nature of his achievement was in his discovering new possibilities of tonal cohesion. In the course of a sonata-form movement, as the music moved into different keys, a delicate balance was set up: on the one hand the composer had to establish each new key sufficiently firmly to allow the listener to feel that he had landed in it, while yet not affirming it so strongly that he should forget the original key from which the music set out.

What we experience depends to a great extent on our musical memories. Perhaps we participate only *in the excitement of actually modulating,* recognizing new events as they happen. We may forget we ever modulated, having arrived in the new key. But an experienced listener might feel an inconclusiveness about a movement unless it ended in the key it had started in and which had been treated as the main, 'home', key. The composer needed to achieve a satisfying balance, with the proportion of time in which the music was in the main key and out of it, while making sure, above all, that there was enough time *to feel* that the music had arrived back in the home key before it ended.

You'll remember we observed how Beethoven's overture *Egmont* consisted of an introductory slow section, followed by a fast section (which we feel to be the main body of the overture), and finally there is a coda. The main body of a sonata movement was conventionally complete in itself, ending with a clear affirmation of the tonal centre by having a recapitulation of the main thematic material all in the tonic key. In the movement by Haydn which was analysed in the *Form and Meaning* units, it was pointed out how the recapitulation had already re-established the home key, only to be given additional emphasis and finality by the coda. In the overture *Egmont* the second half of the recapitulation is *not* in the home key. Having decided to use what Goethe called the 'Victory Symphony' music for the coda, Beethoven may have seen a means of creating a greater dramatic impact by extending the range of tonality covered in the movement, through going away from the tonal centre for part of the recapitulation, then relying entirely on the coda to establish a feeling of tonal repose.

ANSWER TO THE EXERCISE ON PAGE 78

The form of the Rondo may be diagrammatically represented thus:

The cadenza, incidentally, which I have marked in the diagram, is the music you hear close to the end when the violin plays alone for some time. Traditionally the cadenza was improvised by the player, not written in the score by the composer. It served as a kind of musical safety valve which allowed a soloist to release his pent-up energy in an imaginative, unaccompanied solo, before having to toe the line again with an orchestral accompaniment.

(vi) *Piano Sonata in C major, op. 2 no. 3*
Allegro con brio

This is the first movement of the sonata which completes the set of three that Beethoven dedicated to Haydn (see page 8). It is a sonata-form movement.

Listen carefully to identify the three sections of the movement.

The *exposition* ends with a lot of clatter, after a loud passage of rushing octaves followed by two short, thick chords. Look at the score: there is a double bar to mark the end of the exposition and the beginning of the *development*. The latter is not a long section. It ends distinctively with a series of seven repetitions of this

figure ♩♫♫ ♫ (taken from the rhythm of the opening bar of the move-

ment). If you can't see it on the score, bars 136–9, learn this rhythm then listen for it – each statement of the figure begins lower than the previous one. To grasp the rhythm, you might try saying 'going to the OP-ra' quickly, many times! The *recapitulation* begins quietly, after these seven repetitions, and extends to the end.

Listen to the *Allegro con brio* of *Piano Sonata op. 2 no. 3*, which is on the SECOND BEETHOVEN RECORD, side 2 band 1.

Do this before going on

EXERCISE

This time concentrate on the beginning of the movement. For these questions, don't look at the score.

1 Is there an introduction? Do you feel that the movement has started in earnest with important main material in the first bar, or does Beethoven prepare the way for his main material by creating a particular atmosphere before it comes?
2 How much use is made of the material of the opening phrase within the first half minute of the movement?
3 Listen carefully, and count how many times you can hear any phrase obviously derived from the opening one in the first half minute of the movement. How many are there?

Do this before going on

ANSWER

1 No, there is not. This is the main thematic element right at the beginning, brusquely presented without more ado.
2 Extensive use for about twenty seconds, then we hear something else.
3 Six: four phrases derived from it are heard in close succession as the top-line tune, then after a cadence the figure comes twice in the bass line.

If you did not hear this *listen to it again*.

EXERCISE

Listen to the movement right through and follow the score.

Beethoven does something particularly dramatic in the recapitulation. If you bear in mind that a recapitulation is normally a straightforward statement of the material from the exposition, except that it might all be expected to be in the tonic key, you will see that this dramatic stroke is effective because it comes without any warning.

1   What is this dramatic stroke? Give its bar number.
2   What ought we to expect in its place? Unless you are thoroughly familiar with the exposition, you will not remember the order of events, and consequently will not be able to answer this basing it on your experience of listening to it only. If you can read notation, however, it is an easy matter to see it in the music.

Do this before going on

82

38

46

56

64

71

82

91

100

107

118

130

140

153

161

173

182

194

202

213

224

233

234

250

259

ANSWER

1   The dramatic stroke comes at bar 219, where there is a sudden very loud, heavy chord. As this dies away the harmony changes very quietly, and gradually increasing momentum (you will know what I mean when you listen to it) builds up a loud but unstable chord. We feel it has to lead on to a more stable chord, and it does – by way of a short cadenza, or an ornamental flourish at the cadence in a bravura manner.

2   We might expect, if it were an uncomplicated repeat of the exposition, two short chords followed by that passage of quickly played octaves in both hands. It would correspond to bar 84 onward, but transposed into C major.

You might note that in contrast with the very economical slow movement of the piano trio we examined, this fast, early-period piece has a profusion of ideas in it. Both pieces last about the same length of time.

Beethoven was concerned with clearly-defined melodies, themes, as well as small rhythmic cells, in this movement. The difference between main and secondary material was perhaps less obvious than with the piano trio. Note how most of the brilliant virtuoso writing contributes to the secondary material.

You may have commented on the change in the character of the music occurring in the exposition: from an arresting, 'assertive' opening we pass, in contrast, to a more retiring, lyrical section, from bar 27 onward. This is a procedure frequently adopted in sonata-form movements.

Although Beethoven begins the development with a figure he had been working at the close of the exposition, he makes the most stimulating and extensive use of the terse rhythmic figure from the opening.

The cadenza normally found its place in concerto movements, not in sonatas.

That it is here at all draws attention to the bravura character of the sonata.

You have read about most of Beethoven's greatest works in earlier parts of these units, and I have drawn your attention to some characteristics of his style. Let's now take a wider look at his work.

First, how much did he compose? Here is an outline:

32 piano sonatas
     other pieces for piano alone, including the bagatelles and variations, ranging from short easy sets to the mammoth *Diabelli* variations.

songs with piano:
     from the 126 folk song arrangements he made for Thomson to the song cycle, *An die ferne Geliebte*

10 sonatas for violin and piano

5 sonatas for cello and piano

1 sonata for horn and piano

7 piano trios

1 quintet for oboe, clarinet, horn, bassoon and piano

1 septet for strings and wind

1 octet for wind

5 string trios

16 string quartets

the opera, *Fidelio*

the oratorio, *Christ on the Mount of Olives*

2 masses

cantatas

incidental music for the theatre, and a ballet

9 concert overtures

9 symphonies (10, if we include the *Battle Symphony*)

5 piano concertos

1 violin concerto

1 concerto for violin, cello and piano.

It covers all the musical genres of the time. In a summary like this the question is to decide what to omit, since so much of Beethoven's music is played today.

If you have ever sung any of Beethoven's choral music – and the chances are this means either the *Choral Symphony* or his *Missa Solemnis* – you may recall the experience as something of a strain on your voice: so many long passages where you seemed continually to be singing just that much too high to be comfortable, minutes on end at the very top of your range, and loudly too. Those extended sections of sonorous *quiet* music you also sang do not come so quickly to mind. On the basis of the vocal parts in the *Choral Symphony* and the *Missa Solemnis* there is a commonly held opinion that Beethoven could not write for voices. These choral works were not originally as tiring to sing as they are now. Concert pitch (the standard of pitch which all the instruments of the orchestra are tuned to for a performance) was not as high in Beethoven's day. Singers agree, however, that the pitch presently used does make these works extremely taxing, not so much on account of the occasional high notes but because the compass within which they sing for most of the time is so high.

In contrast with the large-scale choral works, some of Beethoven's songs are more simply expressive and lyrical. You might listen, for example, to the setting of *Adelaide* which enjoyed such favour with the public in its own time, and the song cycle *An die ferne Geliebte* ('To the distant beloved').

In working your way through the exercises in this section you have listened to music by Beethoven in three different media: the symphony orchestra, the piano trio and solo piano. Perhaps you have already browsed through the rest of the music on record as well, listening to the operatic chorus, the string quartet movement and more music for piano. Drawing on this, and if you are able to, on your experience of Beethoven's music in general, can you identify the elements which contribute to the distinctive *sound* of Beethoven's music?

As a pointer towards the elements you might think about, read this piece of Hogarth's which, viewing Beethoven's music from the Romantic standpoint of the 1830s, as it does, sees as of greatest significance some of the elements which we are examining now.

> Though he has written little in the department to which Handel devoted all the energies of his mind, yet his spirit, more than that of any other composer, is akin to that of Handel. In his music there is the same gigantic grandeur of conception, the same breadth and simplicity of design, and the same absence of minute finishing and petty details. In Beethoven's harmonies, the masses of sound are equally large, ponderous, and imposing as those of Handel, while they have a deep and gloomy character peculiar to himself. As they swell in our ears, and grow darker and darker, they are like the lowering storm-cloud, on which we gaze till we are startled by the flash, and appalled by the thunder which bursts from its bosom. Such effects he has especially produced in his wonderful symphonies; they belong to the tone of his mind, and are without a parallel in the whole range of music. Even where he does not wield the strength of a great orchestra, – in his instrumental concerted pieces, his quartets, his trios, and his sonatas for the piano-forte, there is the same broad and massive harmony, and the same wild, unexpected, and startling effects. Mingled with these, in his orchestral as well as his chamber music, there are strains of melody inexpressibly impassioned and ravishing ... Of these divine melodies, a remarkable feature is their extreme simplicity ... The music of Beethoven is stamped with the peculiarities of the man. When slow and tranquil in its movement, it has not the placid composure of Haydn, or the sustained tenderness of Mozart; but it is grave, and full of deep and melancholy thought.

(Hogarth, 1838, Vol. 2, pp. 143–4.)

Do this before going on

The lead was Hogarth's reference to Beethoven's broad and massive harmonies, his ponderous, imposing masses of sound, which have a deep and gloomy character.

Think in particular of the sound (isolated if possible from its rhythmic and melodic context), and the impression so often obtained from listening to Beethoven's music is of a very *solid* sound (if one can talk about it as such). The elements concerned are the harmony, and the instrumentation. Here are points to consider, with the examples illustrating them drawn mostly from the music you have on the two gramophone records.

Usually only three or four notes combine to form a chord, which has a particular harmonic function. The harmony is the same, both when the three notes are close together in pitch, and when each of these notes is 'duplicated' an octave higher and an octave lower, making a total of nine different pitches.

Obviously the medium imposes physical limitations on the way the harmony can be presented. A pianist, for example, can't play more notes than the number of keys he can reach with the fingers of two hands – which means that the notes in each handful are bunched closely together.[1] There are greater possibilities when more instruments are involved, and if the harmony were played by the full orchestra, the notes could be spaced further apart. When the notes of the harmony are close together the *sound* isn't the same as when the notes of the

---

[1]Listen for example to the loud, syncopated chords referred to on p. 76, which intrude into the melody close to the beginning of the *Appassionata*: SECOND BEETHOVEN RECORD, side 1 band 1.

chord have been spaced further apart in pitch, e.g. if the bottom note were placed very low down, played by a cello, the next given to a horn in the middle and the top note were played very high in pitch on a piccolo, that chord would sound quite different from, say, the harmony in close position played with one hand on the piano. The choice of instruments or voices involved, and the placing of each note of the harmony in pitch, is fundamental to the quality of the sound that will be produced.

An essential aspect of the art of instrumentation is being sensitive to the qualities of sound each instrument is capable of producing. The compass of most orchestral instruments is about three octaves, and within the total range of pitches an instrument can play are always certain registers in which they sound most attractive. Not unnaturally, most of the music they play is written in these particular registers. Each register has a distinctive colour or tone quality. As a general rule the lowest part of an instrument's compass sounds much fuller, 'darker', and possibly softer, than the upper extreme which, in contrast, may be brilliant but thinner in tone and tenser in feeling. And there may be different registers in the middle which the physical characteristics of the instrument have endowed with other distinctive tonal qualities.

Returning now to Beethoven's broad and massive harmonies, his ponderous, imposing masses of sound; why does his music have this effect?

Unlike most of his contemporaries, whose music usually subscribed to a tune-plus-accompaniment layout, in which the accompaniment conventionally gave just the minimum of harmonic support and rhythmic impetus, Beethoven:

1 made the accompaniment functional in a different way, by allotting to what had traditionally been subordinate parts a greater share of significant melodic material, and

2 gave the accompaniment greater *weight* with a fuller harmony and heavier instrumentation.

Conventionally in late eighteenth-century music most of a listener's attention would have been paid to the tune at the top and the bass underneath, not to the uninteresting parts filling in the harmony in the middle. In realizing the potential of the instruments whose compass naturally condemned them to playing inner parts (being neither capable of playing as high as the normal melody instruments such as the flute, oboe, clarinet and violin, nor as low as the bass, for example the cellos and double basses) Beethoven created a far more versatile orchestral medium, and emancipated certain instruments from subordinate and uninteresting roles. The viola had the most obvious 'promotion'.

In the earliest string quartets of Haydn, 'the tune' tends always to be played by the first violinist, while the other three members of the quartet frequently play uninteresting repeated-figure accompaniments. From 1782 Haydn, and subsequently Mozart, had been exploring the possibilities in string quartet writing of sharing the melodic interest more 'democratically' amongst all four members of the quartet. Beethoven took this up to such an extent that his viola parts become, by the late quartets, very nearly as demanding and full of melodic interest as those of the first violin.

Listen particularly to the closing section of the finale of *String Quartet in E flat major, op. 127*, which is on the FIRST BEETHOVEN RECORD, side 2 band 3.

Do this before going on

The late quartets are technically far more difficult to play than most of Beethoven's orchestral music, and in a composition like the overture *Egmont* or the *Violin Concerto* the violas certainly wouldn't have such a difficult part. Nevertheless, they no longer have the simple accompaniment parts which used to be conventional, and the tone of a strong viola section contributes distinctively to the fullness of the Beethoven sound.

Bassoons had traditionally played the bass line, contributing with the *basso continuo* in Baroque music, then remaining in unison with the cellos for most of the early classical music. They were, therefore, playing interesting lines already, so Beethoven didn't emancipate the bassoon as he had the viola. What he did was to give it a rather more prominent new role as a melodic instrument. He was strongly influenced by Mozart's handling of the wind in his piano concertos and symphonies as well as his writing for them in ensemble music, *Serenades* and other pieces for out-of-door entertainment. If you listen to the use made of the bassoon in the opening passages for wind instruments, in the overture *Egmont* (FIRST BEETHOVEN RECORD, side 1 band 1), or in the *Violin Concerto* (side 2 band 1), particularly in the second episode, you will notice how Beethoven uses the bassoon in just as melodic a manner as any of the other woodwind instruments.

Do this before going on

Listen also to the introduction on the prisoners' chorus 'O welche Lust, in freier Luft', from the finale of Act 1, *Fidelio*. It begins with quiet, low chords played by the strings, widening upward in pitch and increasing in intensity. Having prepared a tense atmosphere appropriate to the dramatic situation, Beethoven could have introduced his chorus in a number of ways. To imply the uncertainty of the prisoners as they emerge out of the dungeon, he makes the vocal parts enter *tentatively*, one after the other; not confidently all together. You will see that there is a 'gap' in the musical situation: between the end of the introduction setting the atmosphere, and when the chorus have all entered and established themselves. To induce us to listen on through this 'gap' Beethoven introduces a melodic figure, which is going to continue as an accompaniment to the chorus. Listen to the bassoon here. It doesn't play a tune in the usual sense, but being so exposed it is certainly what holds your interest for a moment.

Play the FIRST BEETHOVEN RECORD, side 2 band 2.

Do this before going on

Beethoven's cello and double bass parts also have a share of thematic material; not often, but more than was conventional. You have taken note of the fact that the first theme in the fast section of the *Egmont* overture is presented by the cellos (see page 60, and listen to the record) just as the first instruments to play a derivation of the rondo theme after the cadenza in the *Violin Concerto* movement, are the cellos and double basses (side 2 band 1). And if you have listened very perceptively to the string quartet movement, you will have noticed the cello's melodic role. Beethoven's double bass parts are more imaginative than anyone else's before him. If you are familiar with Beethoven's *Fifth Symphony* you may be able to recall the vigorous runs for double bass in the *Scherzo*. There is an active part for double bass in the *Ninth Symphony*, including some highly dramatic passages which Beethoven intended all the cellos and double basses to play together. These passages were regarded as so difficult that, for the first London performances, the leading double bass player then in England, Domenico Dragonetti, was engaged to play them solo. He agreed to do so before seeing the part. Writing to the Philharmonic Society on 21 January 1825, he mentions his mistake:

> I will accept the engagement for the ensuing Season at 10 Guineas per night, and play all the Solos in Beethoven's new Symphony . . . I beg leave to add, that I saw the score of Beethoven last Sunday, and had I seen it before I sent in my terms I would have asked double.
>
> (Willetts, 1970, p. 52.)

The orchestra, as it was when Beethoven came to write for it towards the end of the eighteenth century, had become more or less standard in that most orchestral music was scored for flutes, oboes, clarinets, bassoons, horns and trumpets all in pairs, timpani and strings. Although parts were no longer provided for keyboard instruments, as they had been formerly in Baroque music, the practice of accompanying a symphony or a concerto at the piano continued well on into the early nineteenth century.

The horns, trumpets and trombones Beethoven saw as providing more body in the middle of the orchestral texture, and when called for, incisive, heavy impact (as in the overture *Egmont*). In keeping with his tendency to produce a fuller sound, after reaching the middle period, and although the progression may not be traced in all his orchestral works, it is interesting to see how the traditional pair of horns gives way to three in the *Eroica* (see page 30), and to four in *Egmont* and the *Ninth Symphony*. We have referred to the very high violin part at the end of the overture *Egmont* and the part for a piccolo. This was for special effect. Similarly, in the *Fifth Symphony* Beethoven adds to the standard orchestra a piccolo, a double bassoon and three trombones, while in the *Ninth Symphony* in addition to doubling the traditional pair of horns, he adds a variety of percussion instruments, four vocal soloists and a chorus.

In listening to Beethoven's music you might be aware that there *is* a particular quality of sound which may be identified as Beethoven's, in both his orchestral and his chamber music. It is exciting. And it may be the quality of the sound itself which makes a piece of Beethoven's music appeal to you, as much as the tunes it contains.

Reminder on Assignment

Consult the A202 Course Guide to check on the date your assignment on Beethoven is due. You should not wait until you have completed Section 4.

SECTION 4   LISTENING TO BEETHOVEN'S MUSIC – WITH EMPHASIS ON STYLISTIC DIFFERENCES

Introduction

Figure 24 Beethoven walking, sketch by Johann Peter Theodor Lyser (Staatsbibliothek, Preussischer Kulturbesitz Bildarchiv, Berlin).

In this section you are asked to pay attention to differences of style, which may be *felt* in Beethoven's music. The exercises in the previous section may have helped you establish, or to reinforce, the practice of listening carefully in order to be aware of as much detail as possible in the music. With those exercises, it was usually a straightforward matter deciding whether you had the right or the wrong answer. Now, the matter is not as clear cut. Some characteristics of technique may be pointed out with certainty, but as to the emotional response one might be expected to make to music in a particular style, it would be valueless to suggest what this *should* be.

My aim is to direct you through a particular selection of the music on our gramophone records, in such a way that you will notice points of contrast between them, and come to your own conclusions. These movements are again drawn from different periods of Beethoven's life. It would be useful, as a revision of the biographical material in Section 1, if you referred back to the appropriate pages. Being reminded of the circumstances of a particular composition could have some bearing on the response you made to it.

Decide what the general impression is that you get from each piece of music. Compare the movement in question with the other pieces to which you have just been listening. You'll find it is usually difficult to put into words what the essential difference is. Nevertheless, in doing this, I hope you will open yourself to the music, and enjoy interpreting your response to it. Here are the movements you will be listening to:

(i) '*O welche Lust, in freier Luft*', the prisoners' chorus from Act 1 of *Fidelio*.

(ii) *Piano Sonata in C major, op. 2 no. 3: Allegro con brio.*

(iii) *Piano Sonata in F minor, op. 57*, the *Appassionata: Allegro assai.*

(iv) *Piano Sonata in E major, op. 109: Vivace* and *Prestissimo.*

(v) *Symphony No. 1 in C major, op. 21:* Minuet – *Allegro molto e vivace* (excerpt only).

(vi) *String Quartet in E flat major, op. 127:* Finale.

(i)   '*O welche Lust, in freier Luft*' from *Fidelio*

This male-voice chorus comes in the finale of the first act of Beethoven's only opera, *Fidelio*. Refer to pages 25–8, where the composition of the opera and the difficulties Beethoven had with it, are described. The chorus makes a very powerful dramatic impact, when the prisoners emerge into the light singing what has come to be regarded by some people as a hymn to freedom. It is also seen as a very personal expression of Beethoven's own belief in man's right to freedom:

> Beethoven believed in Freedom and in God, and like many others in his day and ours saw no reason to waste time saying what he meant by these terms. Like many he had felt the impact of the French Revolution. Unlike most his notion of freedom rose quite above political considerations and the local circumstances of his life, although he was interested in politics and freely criticized politicians and the police during a period of Viennese history when it was unwise to do so. His cavalier treatment of sonata conventions reveals a mind which, of its own creative momentum, had broken through previously accepted limitations. A wider background to this is his spontaneous assumption of freedom as a spiritual principle beyond all orthodox religious formulations. For Beethoven, experience of the free spirit which 'bloweth where it listeth' is man's natural, God-given estate, with correlative implications for the conditions of our life here on earth. There are few moments in *Fidelio* more moving than the emergence of the prisoners into the open air for a brief glimpse of daylight. This is symbolic of a general attitude which permeated his entire way of life.
>
> (Arnold and Fortune, 1971, pp. 31–2 (Chapter 1 by Philip Barford,' Beethoven as Man and Artist').)

Listen to this chorus. It is on the FIRST BEETHOVEN RECORD side 2 band 2.

Do this before going on

(ii)   *Piano Sonata in C major, op. 2 no. 3: Allegro con brio*

(iii)   *Piano Sonata in F minor, op. 57*, the *Appassionata: Allegro assai*

To illustrate what I wrote earlier (see page 32) about Beethoven's music taking on a 'heroic' quality, from about the time of the *Eroica* and the two famous piano sonatas the *Waldstein* and the *Appassionata*, listen now to the opening movements of two piano sonatas with which you are familiar already: the *allegro con brio* of the op. 2 no. 3 sonata and the *allegro assai* of the *Appassionata*. Nine or ten years separate these in composition: the op. 2 sonatas date from 1795, the *Appassionata*, started in 1804, was completed two years later.

Listen to the SECOND BEETHOVEN RECORD side 2 band 1, then to side 1 band 1.

Do this before going on

Deciding which of these two movements makes the stronger impression is a personal matter, but it must be agreed, surely, that they are *different*. Whether one chooses to call the *Appassionata* heroic in style is something else.

You may have thought about the technical demands made on the pianist in these sonatas. I wonder which struck you as containing the more brilliant writing? While the *allegro con brio* (op. 2 no. 3) shows the youthful Beethoven making an exhibition of his unquestionable skill at the keyboard, the *allegro assai* of the *Appassionata*, while far more difficult technically, does not give me the impression that Beethoven was concerned with exhibitionism at all. I would think that this is where we come closest to discussing the difference in *spirit* – from the extrovert demonstration of an exceptional piano technique to a serious consideration for the music, the technical means of producing it being incidental.

If you don't feel that there is any difference in spirit between these two movements, listen again and decide whether you agree or disagree with what I've said, before you go on to consider a piano work of the 'late' period.

The piano sonata, as inherited by Beethoven, was conventionally a four-movement piece: the first, a lively sonata-form movement; the second, slow and lyrical; the third a Minuet and Trio; the fourth a dashing Rondo. As early as in his first piano sonatas op. 2, Beethoven had broken with convention, by writing a Scherzo instead of a Minuet in two of the three sonatas of the set. But after the *Appassionata*, there is not one of the eight piano sonatas which follow, in which Beethoven observes what was earlier the standard form.

During the period of his 'late' music, Beethoven was composing relatively few works. But more than half of the ones he wrote are of gigantic proportions – the *Missa Solemnis*[1] and the *Choral Symphony*[1] are obvious instances. The *Piano Sonata in B flat, op. 106*, the *Hammerklavier*[1] as it is called, is another. It preceded them.

Grand in conception and time scale, and utterly uncompromising in its technical demands, it was published in 1819, dedicated to Archduke Rudolph. In it Beethoven's exploration of the piano's tonal qualities is unique – indeed, uncanny when you think that he could not hear aurally the sonorities of the newly enlarged instrument of that period. In marked contrast with his earliest, exhibitionist pieces – like the C major sonata which we have just listened to – the *Hammerklavier* is technically far more demanding but, as we observed in connection with the *Appassionata* sonata, he is here more concerned with the music itself for its own sake, than with showing his exuberance in being fortunate enough to have a virtuoso piano technique.

The *Hammerklavier* is the biggest work of the lean years between 1813 and 1819 when Beethoven composed so little. The only pieces of significance (apart from the revision of *Fidelio*), were two cello sonatas, the song cycle *An die ferne Geliebte*[1] ('To the distant beloved') and three piano sonatas. Discounting his

[1]Excerpts from these are not included on our records.

potboiler, the *Battle Symphony*,[1] he wrote no serious orchestral music, neither symphony nor concerto. So the *Hammerklavier* stands out as, again, a kind of heroic gesture in a period of crisis.

But in the next piano sonata Beethoven composed, the one in E major, op. 109, written the following year, a different spirit may be recognized. Like the *Missa Solemnis* and the *Ninth Symphony*[1] the *Hammerklavier* is an intimidating experience on first confrontation. The question is, how do you react to the E major sonata?

(iv) *Piano Sonata in E major, op. 109*

The complete sonata is played on the record. Listen to the first movement, *Vivace ma non troppo* alternating with *Adagio espressivo*, and the second movement *Prestissimo*.

EXERCISE

Decide whether you feel that the same spirit is expressed in both movements. Describe in a word or two the character of the movements.

Listen to the SECOND BEETHOVEN RECORD side 2 band 2. The first two movements are continuous in this sonata but are clearly discernible because of the character of each.

¹Excerpts from these are not included on our records.

In the op.109 sonata, written between the *Hammerklavier* and the equally colossal *Missa Solemnis* and *Ninth Symphony*, Beethoven achieves great concentration. Notice, in the *Vivace*, there are no link passages, and the two main elements are short and to the point. These are the gentle, rocking figure heard at the beginning and, in contrast, the slow, richly harmonized passage which follows. There is no floundering around, no need for an introduction to get things going, but complete certainty of direction.

I think it has a certain poise about it. The succeeding *Prestissimo* is more forcefully expressed, but not in a 'heroic' kind of way.

If I called it 'serene confidence', you might prefer to describe it as a sense of 'resignation' or 'tragedy'. You are faced with the problem of deciding what the distinction is in the character of each of these three piano sonatas. Finding the right word to convey your meaning is, perhaps an aspect of interpreting it. Here is the opinion of an eminent scholar of keyboard music, Willi Apel:

> It was particularly in the works of his middle period that Beethoven arrived at that style and that musical expression which forever have become associated with his name. Different generations have given different interpretations of this style and expression. During his life-time he was mostly admired for his freedom of inspiration, for his boldness of spirit, for his unbridled flight of fancy. Indeed, to the people who had grown up with ... Haydn, and Mozart, Beethoven was bound to appear as the great liberator, the revolutionary hero. Later, when his innovations had become accepted as the foundation stone of a new era of musical thought, he was celebrated as one of the great leaders of mankind, side by side with Plato, Michelangelo, Shakespeare, and Goethe. His works were felt to be symbols, not so much of heroic daring, but of the eternal ideals of humanity. Today we are inclined to think that such interpretations, though not wholly without significance, do not reveal the full truth about Beethoven, and that his real greatness lies in the purely musical quality of his work. A supreme mastery in handling the problems of musical form and style, a unique power of elaboration and climactic development, an incomparable dynamic quality, an admirable conciseness of language, an inevitable logic of thought – these are some of the most outstanding traits of his musical personality.
>
> (Willi Apel, *Masters of the Keyboard*, Cambridge, Mass., Harvard University Press, 1947, pp. 212–13.)

(v) *Symphony No. 1 in C major, op. 21*
Minuet — Allegro molto e vivace

Having listened to that late-period piano work, you will notice an obvious contrast in style if you now play the excerpt from Beethoven's *First Symphony*. This, you will recall (see p. 73), is the opening of the third movement, *Minuet*.

What do you feel about the difference in style, in particular with regard to the *character* of each, and to the kind of melodic and rhythmic material displayed?

Listen to the FIRST BEETHOVEN RECORD side 1 band 3.

Do this before going on

(vi) *String Quartet in E flat major, op. 127. Finale*

If you are now studying Beethoven's music with the 'innocent ear', you will be in a happier position to approach the late string quartets than the music lover who has often heard terrifyingly erudite things about them. There are, indeed, movements which are difficult on first hearings. But, on acquaintance, there is no doubt that they reward your attention, and there are some movements – particularly slow movements in these quartets – which surely elicit a strong emotional response from all but the most impervious listener.

Beethoven had put off writing his first string quartet until he felt his experience adequate to the task of facing Mozart and Haydn on their own ground (see page 35). Twenty-four years later, in 1822, when he was approached with a commission from a wealthy Russian, Prince Nikolas Borissowitch Galitzin (1794–1860) to compose a string quartet or two, Beethoven welcomed it. It was a spur to induce him back to a genre he had not written in since composing the *String Quartet in F minor, op. 95* of 1810. He promised the first quartet by March 1823, but in fact he was still working on the *Ninth Symphony* that year and well on into the next. Consequently it was not until the later part of the year that he was able to work on it. The work in question *String Quartet in E flat, op. 127* was first performed in 1825 and published the following year, dedicated to Prince Galitzin.

Beethoven turned to the string quartet after the intense effort of completing the *Ninth Symphony*, and the *String Quartet in E flat, op. 127* is a marked contrast in mood, being a less intimidating composition. Having composed this quartet he did not revert to forms requiring large-scale resources (further than sketching a few ideas for a symphony which he never completed). He had found the medium in which he wished to express himself *then*, and for the remaining two and a half years of his life was wholly concerned with work on string quartets, to the total exclusion of anything else of significance. These are not intimate little chamber works, and the fact that he had returned to the medium of the string quartet did not mean that his conception was to be restricted by the traditional view of it. One of the reasons, in fact, why people have found these late quartets tough is that Beethoven seems to them to have over-strained the medium with such powerful music.

When Beethoven had completed the third of these late quartets, the *String Quartet in B flat, op. 130*,[1] Matthias Artaria (the music publisher to whom he had given it) talked him out of his original intention and persuaded him to write a less demanding finale. Artaria thought that the fugue with which the quartet was to have ended, on top of a very long quartet (the first movement being the biggest of Beethoven's quartet movements) would have proved too much even for the most enthusiastic of his admirers. It was therefore published separately and is known as the *Grosse Fuge, op. 133*[1] ('The Great Fugue'). By now we have become more familiar with the style of these late quartets, and the *Grosse Fuge* is often performed as the finale to the *String Quartet in B flat* without causing either the players or the audience to suffer from mental indigestion. But one cannot escape getting a very strong impression of the immense size and scope of the work. In its own way it is another colossus alongside the *Hammerklavier*, the *Missa Solemnis* and the *Ninth Symphony*.

There is little standardization in the late quartets as to the number of movements: the one in E flat op. 127, and the very last, in F major, op. 135, are cast in the traditional four movements; the *Quartet in A minor, op. 132* has five; the quartet mentioned earlier in B flat, op. 130 has six, and the *Quartet in C sharp minor, op. 131* has seven.

You will find an interesting chapter on the late quartets in J. W. N. Sullivan's *Beethoven*, page 136 and onwards. If you are reasonably familiar with the late quartets, it will make sense to you and stimulate you to think about what

---

[1]Excerpts from these are not included on our records.

Sullivan calls the 'spiritual elements' of the music. It will be hard going and you would do well to concentrate on pages 136–8 in particular, if you have not listened to any of the works concerned.

Do this before going on

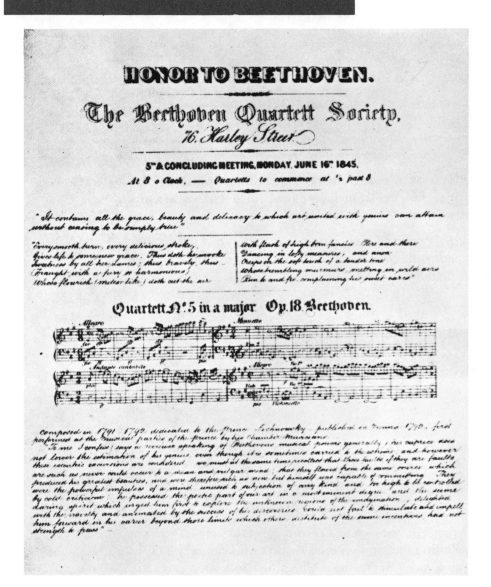

Figure 25 Beethoven Quartet Society Programme, 16 June 1845 (British Museum).

You might be interested to know the background of the concert for which the programme is illustrated in Figure 25. The Beethoven Quartet Society was founded in 1845 by Thomas Alsager of *The Times*, with the object 'of giving the most perfect performance possible of those beautiful compositions'. One may see from the preparations for the Society's first recital, that Beethoven's quartets were held in such respect that the organizers were unwilling to allow just *anybody* to hear them, lest they should fail to appreciate their beauty. Membership would be limited to people who had (according to the prospectus) 'not only a certain rank or station in Society, but a certain knowledge and estimation of the compositions of Beethoven'. At five guineas subscription, there would be five meetings in a session. The first meeting was on 21 April 1845, and at that recital the *String Quartet in E flat, op. 127* was the closing item (Willetts, 1970, pp. 55–6).

The reverence shown towards the late quartets by this society in the nineteenth century was not unique. It continues still, though it may not always be expressed with such lyricism as in a highly-readable guide to the repertoire for amateur string-quartet players, called *The Well-tempered String Quartet* (first published in 1936): 'To any who know these quartets, the written word is superfluous; to such as know them not, words would be meaningless. They are among the things which a man must experience for himself. Playing these quartets is a veritable devotional act of music.' (Bruno Aulick and Ernst Heimeran, *The Well-tempered String Quartet*, London, Novello & Co., 1951, p. 65.)

To emphasize the contrast in style between Beethoven's early and late works, briefly remind yourself again of the *Minuet* from the *First Symphony*, then listen to the *Finale* of the *String Quartet in E flat, op. 127*.

Listen to the quartet movement a number of times. When you have begun to feel that it is familiar, do you think, 'that in this last, enigmatic work by Beethoven are to be found only the ruins of the erstwhile youthful and virile exaltation of his genius'? (*Beethoven, Impressions by his Contemporaries*, p. 187.)

How does it strike you? Is it an approachable or an intimidating piece? Do pay attention in the closing section to that melodic figure which is passed around. What effect does Beethoven create?

Listen to part of the *Minuet* of the *First Symphony*, which is on the FIRST BEETHOVEN RECORD side 1 band 3, then to the *Finale* of the *String Quartet in E flat, op. 127*, also on this record side 2 band 3.

Do this before going on

In conclusion to our Beethoven units, my *envoy*: that after this brief, preliminary inspection of Beethoven's music it may mean rather more to you, and that you may be further inclined to listen to his music when you get the opportunity.

Details of the commercial recordings of Beethoven's music currently available might be of use to you. I don't have much of a record collection myself so I am particularly indebted to Philip Olleson, Research Assistant in Music, the Open University, for writing the Record Supplement which now follows.

Record Supplement

This supplement is in two parts. In the first part I list and recommend complete recordings of the works excerpts of which are on your gramophone records; in the second I deal with recordings of other well-known works by Beethoven.

In the case of Beethoven's best-known works, there are numerous recordings available in a variety of couplings and at a variety of prices. Consequently I make no recommendations for recordings of the symphonies, overtures and piano concertos. *The Gramophone Classical Record Catalogue*, published in March, June, September and December, lists all available recordings at the time of publication, and also indicates the date of the review (if any) in *The Gramophone*. *The Penguin Guide to the Bargain Classics* (London, 1966) is invaluable for picking out recordings which are good as well as cheap, though it is now inevitably somewhat out of date. Record prices change fairly often, but when those quoted here are out of date their relative order ought still to be a useful guide.

Part I

Piano Sonata in F Minor, op. 57 ('Appassionata')

At the time of writing, the 'Appassionata' is available in no less than seventeen recordings, at prices from 79p to £2.39. Best value seems to be the recording made by Alfred Brendel, coupled with the Sonata in E flat, op. 81a ('Les Adieux') and the Sonata in E minor, op. 90. (TV 34116S, 99p). Another coupling – less good to my mind – is with the Sonata in C sharp minor op. 27 no. 2 ('The Moonlight') and the Sonata in D, op. 10 no. 3, which is available in performances by seven artists. Barenboim (HQS 1078, £1.53) is probably the best buy here, though you could try the recordings by Boukoff (SFL 14082, 79p) and Claude Frank (VICS 1596, 99p).

Anton Rubinstein's recording (SBB 6633, £2.28) is coupled with the Sonata in C, op. 2 no. 3, but this is a full-price disc, and if you want recordings of both these sonatas you would probably be better advised to buy them on separate bargain-label records.

Piano Sonata in C, op. 2 no. 3

Again, I recommend Brendel's recording, which is coupled with another early sonata, op. 7 in E flat (TV 34121DS, 99p). Barenboim's recording (HQS 1185, £1.53) is coupled with the Sonata in D, op. 28.

Piano Sonata in E, op. 109

Again, Brendel's recording is excellent value. His performance is coupled with a performance of the Sonata in A, op. 101, and the Sonata in G, op. 49 no. 2 (TV 34111S, 99p). Couplings with another later sonata, op. 110 in A flat, are offered by Charles Rosen (61172, £1.49) and Iso Ellinson (GSGC 14017, £1.49), and with the 'Hammerklavier' Sonata in B flat, op. 106 by Claudio Arrau (SAL 3577, £2.30). The Barenboim medium-price recording is with an early sonata, the one in A, op. 2 no. 2, and the two-movement Sonata in F sharp, op. 78 (HQS 1203, £1.53).

Symphony No. 1 in C, op. 21

As with the 'Appassionata', there is no shortage of recordings here – fifteen at the time of writing. Again, couplings vary, two of the most popular being with the second symphony and with the eighth, although Decca offer Mozart's Symphony No. 36 ('The Linz') on ACL 147 (£1.22).

'Egmont' Overture

You have a recording of the complete overture, of course, but you may be interested in the complete incidental music, available on TV 3426ZS at 99p and on SXL 6465 at £2.27.

Violin Concerto in D, op. 61

Twenty recordings available here. Two cheap recordings are those by Campoli with the London Symphony Orchestra and Krips (EC S 521, 99p) and by Ricci with the London Philharmonic Orchestra and Boult (ACL 5, £1.22). Even cheaper is Kogan with the Paris Conservatoire Orchestra and Silvestri at 87p on CFP 139.

Fidelio

There are six complete recordings to choose from here, some on three records, some on only two. The cheapest is the recording made by Furtwängler in 1954, on HQM 1109 (two records, £1.53 each) – a memorable performance.

There are numerous recordings of the *Fidelio* and *Leonora* overtures, and of excerpts from *Fidelio*.

Piano Trio in D, op. 70 no. 1 ('The Ghost')

The only two recordings currently available are both full price. The Stern-Rose-Istomin Trio's recording (72854, £2.39) is coupled with a performance of the Piano Trio in E flat, op. 70 no. 2; the Beaux Arts Trio offer this trio *and* the Piano Trio in E flat of 1791.

Part II

The Piano Sonatas

Several artists have recorded all the sontas, or nearly all of them. I would recommend the recordings by Alfred Brendel (Turnabout, 99p) and by Daniel Barenboim (HMV, £1.53).

Other Piano Works

Brendel has recorded the complete miscellaneous piano music for Turnabout. I would recommend in particular his recording of the Diabelli Variations (TV 34139S, 99p). The Variations on 'God Save the King' and on 'Rule Britannia' can be found on TV 34162S at 99p.

String Quartets

The Hungarian Quartet, the Amadeus Quartet and the Guarneri Quartet have all recorded the complete quartets, and there are numerous other recordings. The Guarneri Quartet's recordings come in three boxed sets, the individual records of which are not available separately; the Amadeus Quartet offer the records either in boxed sets or individually. The Amadeus recordings are full price, the Hungarian Quartet on HMV are £1.53 and the Guarneri sets work out at £1.10 per record. All the performances are of very high quality, with little to choose between them, so the Guarneri are probably the best buy if you are prepared to buy your Beethoven quartets by the half-dozen; otherwise, the Hungarian Quartet recordings are still excellent value.

The Piano Trios

The complete piano trios have been recorded by the Beaux Arts Trio and by the Stern-Rose-Istomin Trio, both on full-price labels. The 'Archduke' Trio, op. 97, is available in various recordings.

The Septet in E flat, op. 20

Available in three cheap recordings, one by the Vienna Octet (SDD 200, £1.61), one by the Bamberg Symphony Orchestra Chamber Ensemble (TV 34076, 99p) and one by the Consortium Classicum (EXP 29, 95p).

Wind Chamber Music

A particularly attractive recording by the London Wind Soloists includes the Quintet, Sextet and Octet for wind and the Rondino for wind octet (SXL 6170, £2.27).

Lieder

Beethoven's complete Lieder have been recorded by Dietrich Fischer-Dieskau on 139216–18 (3 records, not available separately, £7.05). The song-cycle *An die ferne Geliebte* is available in recordings by Nicolai Gedda (ASD 2601, £2.64) with other Beethoven Lieder and by John Shirley-Quirk (ZRG 604, £2.27) with Beethoven's Gellert songs, and Lieder by Brahms.

The Missa Solemnis

Two cheap-label recordings here. One is by Karajan with the Vienna Philharmonic, the Vienna Singverein der Gesellschaft der Musikfreunde and Elizabeth Schwarzkopf, Christa Ludwig, Nicolai Gedda and Nicolas Zaccaria, re-issued on World Record Club ST 914 (two records, each £1.41). The other is by Kloor, with a far less distinguished cast of soloists on EXP 8–9 (two records, each 95p). On the whole, I recommend the higher-priced version.

In the full-price range, there is another, more recent, recording by Karajan (2707030, £4.70) and one by Klemperer (SAN 165-6, two records, each £2.39).

REFERENCES

Apel, Willi (1947) *Masters of the Keyboard*, Cambridge, Mass., Harvard University Press.

Aulick, Bruno and Heimeran, Ernst (1957) *The Well-tempered String Quartet*, London, Novello & Co.

Arnold and Fortune (1971) (eds.) *The Beethoven Companion*, London, Faber.

de Marliave, Joseph (1961) *Beethoven's Quartets*, New York, Dover Publications.

Fiske, R. (1970) *Beethoven Concertos and Overtures*, B.B.C. Publications.

Hill, R. (1952) (ed.) *The Concerto*, Harmondsworth, Penguin Books.

Hill, R. (1949) (ed.) *The Symphony*, Harmondsworth, Penguin Books.

Hogarth, George (1838) *Musical History, Biography and Criticism*, London, J. W. Parker.

Károlyi, Ottó (1965) *Introducing Music*, Harmondsworth, Penguin Books.

Kerman, Joseph (1967) *The Beethoven Quartets*, London, Oxford University Press.

Kinsky, Georg (1955) *Das Werk Beethovens. Thematisch-bibliographisches Verzeichnis seiner sämtlichen vollendeten Kompositionen*, Munich.

Robertson, Alec (1957) *Chamber Music*, Harmondsworth, Penguin Books.

Robbins Landon, H. C. (1970) *Beethoven*, London, Thames and Hudson.

Rosen, Charles (1971) *The Classical Style*, London, Faber.

Sadie, Stanley (1967) *Beethoven*, London, Faber (Great Composers Series).

Schindler, Anton F. (1966) *The Life of Beethoven*, trans. and ed. Ignace Moscheles (1841) Mattapan, Mass., Gamut Music Co.

Schenk, Erich (1960) *Mozart and his Times*, London, Secker and Warburg.

Schmidt-Görg, J. and Schmidt, H. (1970) *Ludwig van Beethoven*, London, Pall Mall Press.

Scott, Marion (1965) *Beethoven*, London, Dent (Master Musicians Series).

Simpson, R. (1966) (ed.) *The Symphony*, Vol. 1, Harmondsworth, Penguin Books.

Sonneck, O. G. (1967) (ed.) *Beethoven, Impressions by his Contemporaries*, London, Constable (SET BOOK).

Sullivan, J. W. N. (1964) *Beethoven*, London, Allen and Unwin (SET BOOK).

Thayer, A. W. (1967) *The Life of Ludwig van Beethoven*, revised and ed. Elliot Forbes, Princeton University Press.

The Open University (1971) A100 Humanities: A Foundation Course, Units 13–14 *Introduction to Music*, Units 15–16 *Form and Meaning*, Units 27–28 *Mendelssohn's Rediscovery of Bach*, The Open University Press.

Tovey, Donald Francis (1944) *Beethoven*, London, Oxford University Press.

Tyson, Alan (1967) (ed.) *Selected Letters of Beethoven*, trans. Emily Anderson, London, Macmillan.

Valentin, Erich (1958) *Beethoven and his World*, London, Thames and Hudson.

Willetts, Pamela J. (1970) *Beethoven and England*, London, British Museum.

ACKNOWLEDGEMENTS

Grateful acknowledgement is made to the following source for material used in these units:

St. Martin's Press Inc. and Macmillan & Co. Ltd for *Selected Letters of Beethoven*, Emily Anderson (trans.), Alan Tyson (ed.).

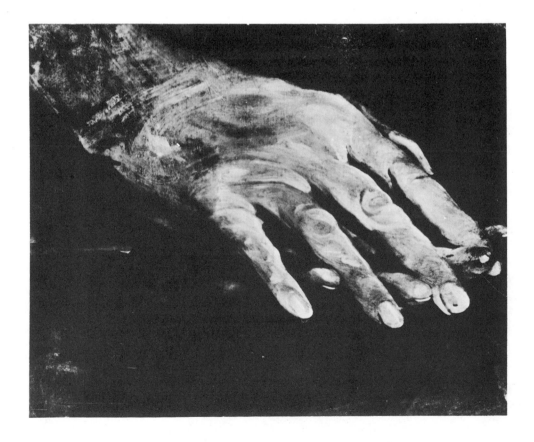

Figure 26 Beethoven's hands, a study by Josef Danhauser (Beethovenhaus, Bonn).

THE AGE OF REVOLUTIONS

A Study Guide to Stendhal's *Scarlet and Black*